Proactive Professional Learning

Proactive Professional Learning

Creating Conditions for Individual and Organizational Improvement

Oran Tkatchov
Mary Tkatchov

ROWMAN & LITTLEFIELD
Lanham • Boulder • New York • London

Published by Rowman & Littlefield
An imprint of The Rowman & Littlefield Publishing Group, Inc.
4501 Forbes Boulevard, Suite 200, Lanham, Maryland 20706
www.rowman.com

6 Tinworth Street, London SE11 5AL

Copyright © 2020 by Oran Tkatchov and Mary Tkatchov

All rights reserved. No part of this book may be reproduced in any form or by any electronic or mechanical means, including information storage and retrieval systems, without written permission from the publisher, except by a reviewer who may quote passages in a review.

British Library Cataloguing in Publication Information Available

Library of Congress Cataloging-in-Publication Data

Names: Tkatchov, Oran, author. | Tkatchov, Mary, author.
Title: Proactive Professional Learning : Creating Conditions for Individual and Organizational Improvement / Oran Tkatchov and Mary Tkatchov.
Description: Lanham : Rowman & Littlefield, [2020] | Includes bibliographical references and index. | Summary: "This book will give an overview of the essential characteristics of effective professional learning"—Provided by publisher.
Identifiers: LCCN 2019039632 (print) | LCCN 2019039633 (ebook) | ISBN 9781475850161 (cloth) | ISBN 9781475850178 (paperback) | ISBN 9781475850185 (epub)
Subjects: LCSH: Professional education. | School improvement programs. | Educational leadership.
Classification: LCC LC1059 .T53 2020 (print) | LCC LC1059 (ebook) | DDC 378/.013—dc23
LC record available at https://lccn.loc.gov/2019039632
LC ebook record available at https://lccn.loc.gov/2019039633

We dedicate this book to our children, Madeline and Alexander, and to the memories of Martha Louise Horne and Alexandre P. Tkatchov.

Contents

Preface		ix
Introduction		xi
1	Why Proactive Professional Learning Is Necessary in Every Profession	1
2	Learning Theory in Professional Learning	7
3	Types of Professional Learning: Choices, Choices, Choices	13
4	Proactive Professional Learning Trait #1: Targeted	17
5	Proactive Professional Learning Trait #2: Data-Driven	21
6	Proactive Professional Learning Trait #3: Job-Embedded	25
7	Proactive Professional Learning Trait #4: Continual	29
8	Conferences and Workshops as Professional Learning	33
9	Observation as Professional Learning	39
10	Book Study as Professional Learning	47
11	Action Learning as Professional Learning	53
12	Individually Guided Learning as Professional Learning	57
13	Mentoring as Professional Learning	61
14	The Proactive Professional Learning Plan: Putting All the Parts Together	67
15	Change and Resistance in Professional Learning	79
Bibliography		87
Index		91

About the Authors ... 93

Preface

Children hold our future in their hands, hearts, and minds. With education, they will become our doctors, nurses, lawmakers, bankers, childcare workers, and various other professionals whose roles have not been conceived of yet. Perhaps because children are our most cherished resource, and their education will ultimately have an impact on all industries and the country's economy, researchers have focused so much on the quality of teacher training and professional development.

Furthermore, the education that we provide our children today will shape their future opportunities to live their best lives, so investment in research-based teacher professional learning that is most likely to lead to improvement in student learning is unquestionably worthwhile. Originally, the main purpose of this book was to pull together in one resource the most relevant information to help school leaders plan a coherent and comprehensive system of professional learning that incorporates the unique needs of their teachers and students with the end goal of improving student learning.

While compiling research, it became apparent that the research surrounding the effectiveness of professional learning for schoolteachers is in essence effective adult learning for continual organizational improvement. Education does not stop after childhood or after entering the workforce. Education continues formally and informally throughout the course of a career and a lifetime.

The lessons from the research can be applied in all industries to promote organizational visions for growth by focusing on another precious resource: the adult learners who want to become better at what they do so that they can make a difference in the world and in their organization. The goal, then, is not to limit the audience of this book to school leaders but to welcome leaders of all types of organizations to transfer these research-based practices to their own context.

To make the information presented in this book not only applicable to school leaders but also to a wider audience, we frequently use general vocabulary such as *enduser* rather than *student* and *organization* rather than *school*. Along with examples from the education profession, we also include additional examples from other industries to illustrate how the concepts can transfer from one industry to the next, all while being mindful of the fact that our area of expertise is limited to education. We, therefore, ultimately leave it up to the reader to envision how the ideas in this book can materialize and take shape in their professional world.

Introduction

Scenario 1

The fire alarm starts blaring and the school's staff know what to do. This is the fourth time they've had a fire drill this school year. They direct students to quietly exit the classrooms and follow the designated path out to the football field, where the rest of their schoolmates are lining up behind orange cones that staff members have placed and monitored according to the emergency plan. The principal is timing the drill from start to finish, with the goal that the whole process is complete two minutes faster than the last drill. Any problems that arise will be discussed with staff at the next staff meeting to find solutions that can be implemented in the next drill.

Scenario 2

In an office of a large organization, an employee reads her emails and notices one from an email address she does not recognize with an urgent message: "You have unused personal time that must be used by the end of the month before it expires. Click here and log in with your company user name and password to view your accrued time and submit a time-off request."

"Oh no," she thinks to herself. "I'm not falling for that this time."

She had been tricked into giving away her password with two similar emails, and both times she received this message from the IT security department: "This was an exercise for the phishing-awareness initiative. Please review the guidelines for identifying and reporting suspicious emails." She was fooled twice despite completing the company's mandatory one-hour workshop and scoring 100% on the quiz that followed. But she had learned from her mistakes and was becoming more adept at detecting an email scam.

Imagine if the individuals in the above scenarios were given only a slide presentation followed by an auto-graded multiple-choice assessment with very limited feedback. Would the school staff who passed the test be ready to successfully follow protocols in the event of an actual emergency? Or would the corporate employee be prepared to avoid a data security breach when confronted with an actual phishing scam?

In both of these scenarios, the professional learning needs of employees in meeting organizational goals (e.g., safety and security) are targeted in authentic, job-embedded exercises that are reinforced with multiple opportunities for practice. Important knowledge and skills are developed beyond one-shot training activities such as a presentation, workshop, or professional conference.

These scenarios show how ongoing, job-embedded practice is necessary for effectively training people to perform new tasks; however, to truly create a culture of continual learning and improvement within an organization, there must also be ample opportunity and support for knowledge sharing among individuals within a professional community. Choice and flexibility are provided for whenever feasible so that individuals can learn and grow in ways that fit within their needs, interests, values, and dispositions.

This book will help organizational leaders develop a larger plan for professional learning that incorporates the needs and goals of the organization, the needs and preferences of the individual learners, and opportunities for individuals to interact with others and apply knowledge in authentic contexts. The choices organizational leaders make about staff development can influence the organization's success. Being proactive and intentional about how professional learning opportunities are selected and incorporated into the learners' professional lives will optimize the benefits for employers, employees, and the students, customers, or clients they serve.

Professional learning is the *processes and activities that can increase the intellectual and relevant knowledge, skills, and attitudes that are related to a profession.* In this book, we have chosen to use the term *professional learning* rather than *professional development* because professional development has traditionally referred to the seminars, workshops, courses, and training sessions for which professionals receive credit either for licensure renewal or advancement.

Inherent in the traditional notion of professional development is a finite time period—the hour, day, or workweek of seat time spent acquiring professional development hours or credits. Professional learning is more appropriate for the purpose of this book because professional learning goes beyond scattered learning experiences that are related to professional duties and obligations. Professional learning is about growing as an individual and participating in knowledge exchange within a professional community.

Chapter One

Why Proactive Professional Learning Is Necessary in Every Profession

"With the right mindset and the right teaching, people are capable of a lot more than we think."—Carol Dweck, *Mindset: The New Psychology of Success*

"Effective leaders understand the value and role of knowledge creation, they make it a priority and set about establishing and reinforcing habits of knowledge exchange among organizational members."—Michael Fullan, *Leading in a Culture of Change*

In America, the average person will spend 90,000 hours at work, or about a quarter of his or her adult life. Job satisfaction, then, can have an enormous influence on quality of life. Unfortunately, many in the workforce will spend all or a portion of their work life feeling stagnant and lacking passion for their job. Some studies show that as many as 89% of workers are not passionate (as defined by being committed, challenged, and connected) about what they do (Hagel, Brown, & Samoylova, 2013). This statistic has negative implications not only for the individuals who feel disengaged and unmotivated at work but also for their employers.

In the book *Leading Change* (2012), John Kotter, renowned expert on organizational leadership and change, wrote of today's world, "A globalized economy is creating both more hazards and more opportunities for everyone, forcing firms to make dramatic improvements not only to compete and prosper but also to merely survive" (p. 20). Organizations in all sectors—from education to non-profit to business to medicine—have vision statements that express a future ideal as well as short-term goals for incremental and continual improvement. For the organizational improvement goals to be achieved, individuals within the organization must develop their knowledge and skills in ways that align with the common organizational goals in addition to their personal interests.

There are numerous benefits to having thoughtfully planned systems for professional learning within an organization:

1. *You increase the collective knowledge of your team.* When continuous learning and collaboration are expected, the collective knowledge of the system's workforce continues to grow. In a survey titled "The State of American Jobs," 87% of workers surveyed believed it will be critical for them to get training on new job skills during their career in order to remain relevant in the workplace (Pew Research Center, 2016).
2. *You boost employees' job satisfaction and productivity.* Research shows that there is a significant impact of professional learning on employee retention. It has already been established that there is a relationship between job-embedded professional learning and workplace effectiveness, and 77% of employees in highly effective workplaces stated that they are more likely to remain at their current workplace, compared with 30% of employees who work in places with low levels of workplace effectiveness (Society for Human Resource Management, 2016). Additional studies show that not only does offering professional learning increase retention, but it increases employee trust in the organization.
3. *You make your company more appealing to the current workforce.* A 2016 Gallup Poll showed that almost 60% of millennials surveyed answered that opportunities to learn and grow are extremely important when looking for a company to work for (Gallup Institute, 2016).
4. *You attract the right kind of in-demand candidates.* Having a focused plan for company improvement and growth attracts candidates with similar passions. When an organization offers professional learning opportunities, employees who strive to learn and constantly improve will be enticed to apply.
5. *You make succession planning easier.* When changes in personnel are needed due to organizational growth, retirements, and employee turnover, continually growing employees from within can prepare internal candidates to step up since they will already have some of the knowledge and skills needed to fill these positions.

When part of a larger plan, professional learning can be an important tool in driving organizational improvement. However, haphazardly spending money on professional learning activities for employees without having a well-developed strategy for implementation of learning on the job is not by itself effective in making employees more competent.

Take American public schools as an example. Based on the findings of a two-year study conducted by The New Teacher Project, the largest 50 school districts in the United States spend around $8 billion a year on professional development for teachers. The findings also showed that "despite enormous and admirable investments of time and money, most teachers we studied do not appear to be improving substantially from year to year" (The New Teacher Project, 2015). Merely spending money on professional learning experiences is not enough to make a significant difference in teacher effectiveness. There must be a proactive and coherent strategy behind professional learning decisions.

PROFESSIONAL LEARNING AND ORGANIZATIONAL EFFECTIVENESS

The individual's needs and goals for personal and professional growth are inextricably connected to the performance of an organization. The Society for Human Resource Management (SHRM) identified seven dimensions of a highly effective workplace:

1. Provide learning opportunities as a part of everyday work life.
2. Create a culture where supervisors support the job success of their teams.
3. Be mindful of the positive and negative repercussions of autonomy.
4. Foster workplace belongingness.
5. Support a culture of work-life fit.
6. Improve advancement systems.
7. Recognize and reward the importance of supportive co-worker relationships.

The first dimension of an effective work environment is the presence of job-embedded professional learning opportunities. The other dimensions focus on individual needs: the need to be supported and encouraged to achieve, the need to have self-direction and ownership while also being part of a community in which peers share ideas and expertise, and the need to feel recognized for accomplishment. A good professional learning plan can incorporate multiple dimensions of an effective work environment.

The topic of this book, proactive professional learning, is a way to create a rewarding, highly effective work environment that makes people want to get the most out of their work experience and, in doing so, optimize the effectiveness of the organization that employs them.

WHAT IS PROACTIVE PROFESSIONAL LEARNING?

Being proactive means preparing for something ahead of time. It is to see the potential that change and growth can bring and make preparations for achieving that potential rather than waiting until problems arise to act in response. To be proactive in creating a professional learning plan for an organization, various factors must be considered and synthesized into a cohesive context for worker development: the goals and priorities of the organization; the skills that are needed now and in the future to achieve organizational goals; the qualities of the adult learners that will influence their desire, motivation, and capacity to learn; the learning delivery options for developing and reinforcing the desired knowledge and skills; and the potential for peers to participate in knowledge creation and maximize the benefits of professional learning.

What Does Professional Learning Look Like in High-Performing Organizations?

The goal of this book is primarily to show how lessons from studies of teacher professional learning can be applied to support adult learners in all other industries to drive continual improvement in any organization. The traits of effective professional learning will be discussed in Chapter 3, but first it is necessary to look at commonalities among high-performing school systems internationally that have successful, well-developed professional learning designs.

While studying high-performing school systems in Shanghai, Hong Kong, Singapore, and British Columbia, researcher Ben Jensen identified five components that these effectively functioning systems shared (Jensen, Sonnemann, Roberts-Hull, & Hunter, 2016):

1. *Effective professional learning design that reflects adult learning principles is at the core of organizational improvement efforts.* High-performing systems set clear and deliberate directions for quality professional learning as a means for system-wide improvement. The tenets of adult learning theory, discussed in more detail in Chapter 2, are fundamental when professional learning opportunities are being planned and implemented.
2. *Designated roles for leading professional learning are established throughout the system.* Official peer leaders among the staff within the system are tasked with ensuring that effective professional learning practices are used to meet organizational goals. These leaders are master practitioners who serve as role models for their colleagues, and

they serve as program designers, facilitators, mentors, and trainers of other experts and potential leaders within the organization.
3. *The system recognizes the development of professional expertise.* As individual staff grow their expertise, effective systems acknowledge their achievements as criteria for promotions and other opportunities for recognition. Professional learning is an indicator of success for leaders and staff.
4. *Staff and leaders share responsibility for personal professional learning and the learning of others.* Accountability for professional learning is reinforced through employee evaluations, which are directly tied to promotions, as well as cultural expectations within the system. Peers expect one another to participate in collaborative professional learning. Leaders in the system regularly review data to evaluate the effectiveness of the professional learning strategies of the system as a whole and use the data to make decisions for which the decision-makers are held accountable. The data includes input from multiple stakeholders (e.g., parents, students, teachers, and leaders).
5. *Time is provided in the workday for collaborative professional learning.* Separating professional learning from the professional day is inefficient and disconnected from authentic practice. In effective systems with high-quality professional learning, the learning is an important part of the workday, and collaboration is expected as a professional duty. Work policies free up time for employees to engage in collaborative professional learning.

These examples of effectively operating a continually improving system demonstrate the importance of having a strategic, coherent plan for professional learning. A proactive professional learning plan (PPLP), described in depth in Chapter 14, is a system that combines what research shows to work in professional learning and implementation science. This plan will help organizations in any industry implement professional learning in ways that will support sustained improvement for an organization as a whole and the adult learners within it. Everything that is built will eventually need adjustment or improvement; the PPLP helps leaders anticipate what is needed to keep improving the professional learning within an organization.

Chapter Two

Learning Theory in Professional Learning

"Learn from yesterday, live for today, hope for tomorrow. The important thing is to not stop questioning. Curiosity has its own reason for existing."—Albert Einstein

"Now I remembered that the real world was wide, and that a varied field of hopes and fears, of sensations and excitements, awaited those who had courage to go forth into its expanse, to seek real knowledge of life amidst its perils."—Charlotte Brontë, *Jane Eyre*

Think of one of your strongest skills, a skill that is essential to your effectiveness as a professional. How and why did you develop that skill? Most likely, you were motivated to develop that skill because you saw a need for it or were passionate about the work it would help you to perform. Chances are, as an adult you also had some background knowledge or prior experience that you could connect the new learning to and make sense of it.

Since the purpose of investment in professional learning activities is to strengthen the knowledge and skills of adult workers so that they are more effective in performing their jobs or the jobs they would like to grow into, decisions about professional learning should be based on research on how people, particularly adults, learn. Professional learning activities that are not grounded in current theory about learning and change are not as likely to lead to sustained change in professional practice or result in the benefits that evidence-based professional learning can produce.

Chapter 2
ADULT LEARNING THEORY

Malcolm Knowles is known as the father of *andragogy*, or "the art and science of helping adults learn" (Knowles, 1970). Knowles's andragogical model is built around six assumptions about—or characteristics of—the adult learner (Knowles, Swanson, & Holton, 2005):

1. Adults need to know why they are learning something new before they begin to learn it. They need to understand the purpose of the learning and how they will benefit from it.
2. Adults need to be treated as though they are capable of taking responsibility for their own learning. Because they have a *self-concept* of being independent, adults will resist learning situations in which they feel as though they have no control over or choice in what and how they learn.
3. Adults will bring a wide range of life and learning experience into learning situations. The adult learners' experiences can be the "richest resources for learning," serving as anchors on which to build new knowledge, but they can also be sources of bias and obstacles to different ways of knowing.
4. Adults enter learning situations ready to learn knowledge and skills that are necessary for and relevant to their stage of life or career development. Adults tend to be open to learning when they believe it will promote their personal or professional growth.
5. Adults have a problem- or task-centered orientation to learning. Orientation refers to the relative position of something or someone (the learner) to something else (the learning). The learning is more relevant and meaningful to adults when it will help them to solve a real-world problem or perform an authentic task.
6. Adults are more motivated by internal factors than external. While external factors such as a promotion or salary increase can serve as motivators for learning, the strongest motivators for adult learning reside within the learner, such as the desire to make a difference, improve oneself, or achieve greater work-life satisfaction.

So if we know adults are self-directed, experienced, ready, problem-centered, and internally motivated, then how do employers proactively plan for learning experiences that will most likely lead to permanent and positive growth for working adults? Sometimes it might be necessary for the employer to choose the knowledge and skills that staff are required to learn and the manner in which they learn them; however, the six assumptions of the adult learner can be incorporated into the design of mandatory learning experiences to maximize their effectiveness with diverse adult learners.

For example, learning experiences should be designed around clear, meaningful goals and benefits that are transparent to the learners. Trainers should communicate and reinforce the benefits of the learning for the individuals and the organization and describe the problems that can be solved using the new knowledge and skills. Also, learning experiences should include problem-solving and real-world application, since adult learners need to see how the learning will be applied in their real-life work roles.

But ultimately what adult learning theory teaches us is that choice should be built into the learning opportunities as much as possible if we want willing and motivated adult learners who will drive organizational improvement. Consider how this ubiquitous quote from Steve Jobs applies to professional learning: "It doesn't make sense to hire smart people and tell them what to do; we hire smart people so they can tell us what to do." The decision-makers will not always have the answers to all the problems, nor will they have even identified all of the potential problems. So how can they determine what all of the professional learning needs are or will be? When the professional learning plan within an organization includes no opportunity for self-directed learning, the organization is stunting its own growth. If given the opportunity, individuals at all levels of the organizational hierarchy will identify workforce learning needs that will enable the organization to stay ahead of the game, and they will seek out and share that knowledge on their own.

Chapter 3 gives an overview of the various options for professional learning delivery so organizations can plan for different learning modes and supports from which the individual learners may choose, depending on the needs, goals, and capacity of the organization to provide those opportunities.

THEORIES OF SOCIAL LEARNING

In *Leading in a Culture of Change* (2001), Michael Fullan writes, "If you remember one thing about information, it is that it only becomes valuable in a social context. . . . Leading in a culture of change does not mean placing changed individuals into unchanged environments. Rather, change leaders work on changing the context, helping create new settings conducive to learning and sharing that learning" (p. 79). The message here is that to see real change from investments in professional learning, organizations need to be focused on creating a culture of learning in which individuals share their expertise and support the growth of others in a perpetual "knowledge exchange."

Lev Vygotsky's theory of sociocultural development gives us insight into why the social context of learning is important because it emphasizes the critical role of social interaction in human learning. According to Vygotsky's theory, a learner constructs knowledge through interaction with a "More

Knowledgeable Other" (MKO), someone with a higher understanding and ability than the learner.

The MKO guides the learner through modeling and cooperative or collaborative dialogue until the learner is able to independently perform the task. Sociocultural development theory supports cooperative learning configurations in which peers are allowed to learn from one another, the more skillful peers taking on the role of the MKOs. The MKO does not need to be in a formal training position or position of authority.

Psychologist Albert Bandura's social learning theory, also called social cognitive theory, shares Vygotsky's premise that people learn from observing and interacting with others. Bandura's theory has four components: attention, memory, imitation, and motivation. For a learner to learn through observation, he or she must pay attention to the observed behavior, remember what was observed, be able to imitate observed behavior, and then be motivated to repeat it at a later time. However, simply learning through observation does not automatically mean that a person will perform the observed behavior if there is no motivation to repeat it. People often observe behaviors that they do not imitate. This is why instructors and organizational leaders will benefit from awareness of the factors that motivate their adult learners (refer back to adult learning theory).

SELF-EFFICACY

Albert Bandura is also well known for his concept of *self-efficacy*, which is a person's belief in his or her own ability to learn or accomplish a goal. Bandura's research led to his theory that people's sense of self-efficacy influences their success at a task; they will be more persistent and expend more effort on tasks they know they can accomplish and are, therefore, more likely to accomplish them. Conversely, people will avoid or put less effort into tasks when they believe they are not likely to succeed. Some organizations are now focusing on promoting employees' sense of self-efficacy, as are teachers with their students, because of its effect on learning.

Scenario 1

A new staff member, Janea, receives an email from her manager that includes instructions to learn about a file-sharing application that the organization uses for staff to be able to work on digital documents at the same time. The email includes a link to a training document and short video that demonstrates the process of locating, creating, sharing, and editing documents in the application.

Scenario 2

A new staff member, Janea, receives an email from her manager that includes instructions to learn about a file-sharing application that the organization uses for staff to be able to work on digital documents at the same time. The email includes a link to a training document and short video that demonstrates the process of locating, creating, sharing, and editing documents in the application. The manager also writes that Mario, a team member with the same title who has been with the organization for two years, will be setting up a meeting to work with Janea on learning the application.

Mario meets with Janea. He walks her through the steps presented in the training document and video and shares his own "lessons learned" from using the application on the job. Mario then watches as Janea performs the steps, intervening and reteaching when necessary. Mario explains how certain organizational tactics that he developed over time through trial and error and using Internet research have saved him a lot of time and frustration. He tells Janea to try it on her own and then come to him with questions—or even suggestions for improvement—if the need arises.

Compare the two scenarios and ask yourself these questions:

1. Which employee would you rather be?
2. As an employer, which training situation would you prefer?

Scenario 1 demonstrates simply a transfer of information and an expectation that it be "learned," whether or not the vehicle for learning is actually effective. Scenario 2, on the other hand, demonstrates knowledge sharing among peers and an openness to co-create new knowledge in ways that benefit the employees through increased job satisfaction and the employer through improved efficiency. It also shows that the knowledge is not fixed and finite—that even better options for using the application on the job might emerge after a new person, with new insights and perspectives, engages in the conversation.

SUMMARY: PUTTING IT ALL TOGETHER

What learning theory teaches us is that building the professional capacity of workers involves more than information transfer and acquisition. The goal of a professional learning plan is figuring out (1) how to establish an environment that promotes collaborative knowledge creation and knowledge sharing at all levels of the organization, (2) how to maximize the benefits of professional learning so that it is successful in building capacity among staff, and (3) how to reasonably provide staff with choices in professional learning opportunities and the supports they need to help them successfully implement their learning on the job.

Chapter Three

Types of Professional Learning

Choices, Choices, Choices

"Until a person can say deeply and honestly, 'I am what I am today because of the choices I made yesterday,' that person cannot say, 'I choose otherwise.'"—Stephen R. Covey, *7 Habits of Highly Effective People*

"Imagine a world in which the vast majority of us wake up inspired, feel safe at work and return home fulfilled at the end of the day."—Simon Sinek

MEETING ORGANIZATIONAL GOALS BY FOCUSING ON INDIVIDUAL LEARNER NEEDS

When organizational leaders plan for professional learning for staff, they have a number of questions to answer. What knowledge and skills will we prioritize? How will the learning be delivered? Will staff attend a face-to-face training? Will they complete an online workshop? Could there be a combination of training methods? Finally, how can we ensure that the learning is being implemented on the job? So many questions to answer and choices to make.

When creating a proactive professional learning plan, an important perspective about employee motivation needs to be considered. This perspective is expressed in organizational theorist Douglas McGregor's Theory Y, a theory of management styles based on the assumption that people are self-motivated and will strive to achieve organizational goals when they are aligned with their own goals for professional fulfillment. The opposing theory is Theory X, which is based on the assumption that employees by nature will be unmotivated and they need to be controlled by management to be productive.

Explaining the role of management in Theory Y, McGregor writes, "The essential task of management is to arrange organizational conditions and methods of operation so that people can achieve their own goals best by directing their own efforts toward organizational objectives. This is a process primarily of creating opportunities, releasing potential, removing obstacles, encouraging growth, providing guidance" (McGregor, 1960, p. 350).

This is the essential goal of a proactive professional learning plan: to map out ways to establish the "conditions and methods of operation" that will encourage and support employees in meeting their individual goals and needs for professional fulfillment while simultaneously working toward the organization's objectives. Knowing the traits that make professional learning effective and the range of options available for professional learning experiences empowers organizational leaders to create opportunities for employees to release their potential to learn and grow.

CHARACTERISTICS OF EFFECTIVE PROFESSIONAL LEARNING

The characteristics of effective professional learning described in this chapter come from research about teacher professional development and learning, but the findings can be applied to multiple industries and contexts since we are looking at what helps adults become more knowledgeable and competent professionals. A synthesis of research shows that effective professional learning has these main traits:

1. It is *targeted*. Targeted professional learning is focused on a specific need or needs. For example, "We need additional learning in the area of technology" is not targeted. A more targeted professional learning goal is, "We need all teachers to be proficient in using online tools to communicate with families."
2. It is *data driven*. The topic for professional learning, or the problem of which the learning is to help solve, is based on data showing a need. Possible data points to analyze and inform professional learning needs include student or client data, market forecasts, test results, observation data from informal walk-throughs, formal evaluations, survey data, and employee perception data.
3. It is *job-embedded*. Opportunities to apply the learning are built into the workday and rooted in day-to-day work practices. Collaboration with colleagues is leveraged and supported whenever possible.
4. It is *continual*. The learning does not stop at the end of a course or workshop. When employees have regular and recurring opportunities

to apply the targeted skills, the learning has a better chance of improving employee practices long term. The learners should also be continually receiving constructive feedback and tracking or reflecting on their own progress.

These four areas are described in detail in Chapters 4, 5, 6, and 7.

PROFESSIONAL LEARNING MODELS

Professional learning models are the ways in which formal and informal learning opportunities are delivered or experienced. There is a wide variety of professional learning models beyond the typical workshop or training. These models can be situated in learning environments that are face-to-face, online, or hybrid (a combination of both), and they can be synchronous (when all participants learn at the same time) or asynchronous (when participants learn at their own pace and on their own time).

Learning Forward, a professional association dedicated to educator professional learning, calls these delivery models "learning designs." Learning Forward highlights the potential for drawing on multiple models or learning designs to individualize the learning experience: "Learners and facilitators of learning may weave together multiple designs within on-site, online, or hybrid learning to achieve identified goals and to differentiate learning designs to meet the unique needs of individual learners" (Learning Forward, 2017).

- *Workshops and conferences*: Courses, trainings, and presentations can occur either in-person, online, or in a hybrid model. Topics can be covered either asynchronously or synchronously to multiple participants at once. See Chapter 8.
- *Observation*: Participants observe and are observed by a peer. Observations are collaborative and include taking notes, asking questions, and giving feedback on performance. The participants' reflections then drive the change in practice. See Chapter 9.
- *Book study*: Participants (a group of colleagues) study a book that will help them to develop their professional expertise. Participants meet to discuss the book and reflect on how it applies to their work and how it will help them to improve as professionals. See Chapter 10.
- *Action learning*: Participants research a problem of practice and use the findings to plan change. See Chapter 11.
- *Individually guided learning*: Participants identify an area of focus for professional growth and select activities to foster their own self-directed learning. See Chapter 12.

- *Mentoring*: Less experienced participants are matched with an expert to develop a mutually beneficial relationship that will lead to a sharing of ideas and growth for both the mentor and the mentee. See Chapter 13.

PROFESSIONAL LEARNING: NOT ALWAYS A TOP-DOWN ENDEAVOR

If we learn anything from McGregor's Theory Y, we know that plans for professional learning do not always need to come from management. Staff, through their own desire to become more competent and satisfied professionals, can provide input about what their professional learning needs are and organize their own learning experiences.

For example, an organization might have a clearly communicated priority of becoming more client-centered. Employees might request to attend conferences, webinars, and workshops to learn about various ways to better meet the needs of their clients. They might organize their own book studies or action-learning projects to complement organization-wide trainings and extend their learning. As long as leadership is open to input from staff and able to work with staff on aligning the desired learning activities and experiences with organizational goals, employee-driven professional learning can be effective and rewarding and it can contribute to the culture of learning within an organization.

Chapter Four

Proactive Professional Learning Trait #1

Targeted

"When I have a higher purpose, I find the energy and the courage to go outside my comfort zone and to learn in a deep way."—Robert Quinn

"Work takes on new meaning when you feel you are pointed in the right direction. Otherwise, it's just a job, and life is too short for that."—Tim Cook

You may have seen a bumper sticker that reads, "Not All Who Wander Are Lost," a line from J. R. R. Tolkien's *The Lord of the Rings* that found its way onto the vehicles of avid travelers. It is a fitting sentiment for going on an adventure, but it is not a compatible mindset for engaging in proactive professional learning. The first trait of effective professional learning is that it is focused and targeted; it has clearly defined learning goals for improving professional effectiveness. It should be clear to participants (and their employers) what they should know and be able to do as a result of the learning.

Below are examples of professional learning goals:

- "Teachers write essential questions at each level of Bloom's Taxonomy."
- "Participants will correctly explain the differences between the new tax codes and the old tax codes."
- "Learners will demonstrate data-analysis strategies for identifying potential market changes."
- "Staff will demonstrate how to use the new informed-consent form in patient care."

In addition to helping employers and learners make informed professional learning decisions, clearly stated learning goals improve the chances that the professional learning will be effective. Recall the discussion about adult learning theory in Chapter 2. Since adults need to know why they are learning something before they put in the effort to learn it, well-articulated learning goals can provide answers to the questions What am I going to learn? and Why am I learning it? Transparent learning goals can provide the purpose and relevance that adults need to be motivated to learn.

A DISCUSSION ABOUT TERMINOLOGY

This book uses the term *learning goal* to refer to the whole body of terminology used to describe the desired results from a training or professional learning experience. Learning goals can have many names: learning outcomes, learning objectives, learning targets, and competencies, just to name a few. Some trainers or institutions will use them interchangeably; however, there are some nuances, and it helps to know the differences when planning for professional learning.

Learning objectives or *learning outcomes* might be used to refer to the knowledge and skills that learners should demonstrate either by the end of a lesson or the end of a whole course or training program—they are the objectives for learning or the desired outcomes of the learning.

Learning targets is used to specifically refer to short-term learning goals—such as chunks of related information to be learned in a single lesson within a multi-day or multi-week class. Learning targets are a means for instructors and learners to track and measure learner progress toward meeting larger, long-term learning goals.

The word *competency* has also been used interchangeably with *learning objective* or *outcome*, but the distinction is that competency has an emphasis on *application* of knowledge in a real-world situation. In professional learning, competency refers to a set of skills and abilities that a competent professional would *demonstrate* on the job in a common professional situation. Since a competency expresses higher levels of knowledge and performance, it can be made up of several smaller learning objectives that, combined, lead up to mastery of the competency. This distinction shows why courses or training programs that include competencies also have learning objectives, targets, or outcomes. See the examples in Table 4.1.

When evaluating professional learning opportunities to determine whether they are worth the investment, organizational leaders are wise to consider whether the stated learning goals are aligned with organizational goals. Individuals should also examine stated learning goals to determine whether a professional learning opportunity meets their own learning needs for becom-

Table 4.1. Competency Examples

Teaching	*Competency:* The teacher modifies lesson plans based on student learning data to accommodate diverse learners' needs.	This competency requires the (competent) teacher to apply a combination of skills and abilities including collecting and interpreting student learning data, knowing different strategies for modifying lesson plans, and being able to determine when those modification strategies are appropriate.
Business	*Competency:* The sales executive creates a marketing plan that is tailored to an organization's mission, portfolio of products and services, and identified target audience.	This competency requires the (competent) business professional to apply a combination of skills and abilities including researching an organization, identifying a target audience, knowing the components of an effective marketing plan, and tailoring written communication to a specified audience.
Nursing	*Competency:* The nurse prioritizes patients for medical treatment based on their vital signs and physical symptoms.	This competency requires the (competent) nurse to apply a combination of skills and abilities including taking a patient's temperature, blood pressure, and pulse; knowing what symptoms indicate serious illness or condition; and demonstrating proper procedures for prioritizing patients based on a synthesis of the collected input.

ing more competent professionals. A proactive professional learning plan prioritizes learning experiences that are targeted and focused on the skills that will best support staff in solving the most pressing work-related problems and helping the organization progress toward its mission and vision.

Chapter Five

Proactive Professional Learning Trait #2

Data-Driven

"The goal is to turn data into information and information into insight."—Carly Fiorina

"I believe in evidence. I believe in observation, measurement, and reasoning, confirmed by independent observers. I'll believe anything, no matter how wild and ridiculous, if there is evidence for it. The wilder and more ridiculous something is, however, the firmer and more solid the evidence will have to be."—Isaac Asimov, *The Roving Mind*

An organization puts significant resources into professional learning and training as an investment in its future. If money, time, and employee energy are spent on professional learning that does little or nothing to improve the organization, then those resources are wasted. Proactive decisions about professional learning are based on data. Data-driven decisions occur at four major points in the cycle:

1. *Setting a baseline and identifying needs*: Data should be analyzed to answer the questions Where are we now? and What do we need to be better? Here data are used to identify not only problems but also potential causes of the problems. The topics and goals for professional learning, or the problems that the learning could help solve, are based on data showing that staff development is needed.

   It is important to solicit staff input when determining needs. Not only is staff input essential for accurately identifying areas for professional development, but it will help to gain their buy-in for professional learning efforts. When staff feel like they have been part of the decision-making process, they will be more willing to engage in and implement the learning on the job.

2. *Adopting learning models, methods, and resources*: In this area, data are used to answer the questions What models/methods/resources have proven to be effective in meeting these learning needs? and What evidence-based strategies and programs can help us meet our learning and improvement goals? Staff input is beneficial here as well since they know what their learning preferences are and should be given choices and supports when feasible.

3. *Monitoring implementation of learning*: Once professional learning has taken place or is in progress, data should be collected to determine whether staff are achieving mastery of the learning and correctly implementing the learning in professional practice. These data will help organizational leaders know whether staff members need additional training or supports to successfully implement their learning on the job.

4. *Evaluating the results of the learning*: The data in this phase should indicate to what degree staff and the end users (students, clients, patients, etc.) benefited from the professional learning being implemented in practice. Data about the end results can also help to make informed decisions about what should be done differently next time or what additional staff development is needed to obtain the desired results for staff and the end users. These data can also be shared with staff to either reinforce the progress they have made or, if improvement is needed, to serve as motivation for and justification of further learning. Thomas Guskey (2013), an authority on teacher professional development evaluation, notes:

> Some educators understand the importance of evaluation for event-driven professional development activities, such as workshops and seminars, but forget the wide range of less formal, ongoing, job-embedded professional development activities—study groups, action research, collaborative planning, curriculum development, structured observations, peer coaching, mentoring, and so on. But regardless of its form, professional development should be a purposeful endeavor. Through evaluation, you can determine whether these activities are achieving their purposes. (p. 2)

Data can be collected in many ways, depending on the type of information that is needed. *Quantitative data* provides information about quantities and can be measured in or converted into numbers. Some sources of quantitative data for determining professional learning needs include test scores or results, sales or enrollment numbers over time, analytics of website traffic, and financial records. Consider these examples of information derived from quantitative data:

> The ratio of students to teachers at this school is 32:1.
> We attract 50% of our customers from online advertising.
> Our patients spend an average of 2.4 days in the hospital.

Qualitative data provides information about quality, and while it cannot be measured in the same way that quantitative data can, it can be just as informative and useful. Qualitative data can be collected using surveys of end users and employees, interviews, and observations.

Consider these examples of information derived from qualitative data:

> Based on the complaints that the district office has received from parents, teachers are not adequately communicating with parents about student progress.
> Based on formal classroom observations, many teachers are not clearly aligning lessons with state academic standards.
> An analysis of recorded customer service calls shows that the instructions that come with the product are too confusing.
> Patient surveys show that our patients are frustrated with a perceived lack of empathy from staff.

Multiple sources of data—a combination of quantitative and qualitative—should be used to determine professional learning needs and goals for an organization. Furthermore, there are multiple types of data sets, including *performance data*, *perception data*, and *process data*.

- Performance data, which are data used to track performance and are focused on results, could include sales numbers, student achievement data, work tickets closed, or client retention. Performance data will indicate how well staff or the organization as a whole is achieving goals or its purpose.
- Perception data show what people think—their attitudes and beliefs—about the organization or what is being accomplished and how well. Perception data can be collected from staff, clientele, or community focus groups, surveys, or online ratings and comments.
- Process data provide evidence about the processes used to achieve results. Process data help to answer these questions: What was done? What procedures were followed? Which steps were efficient and which steps did not go as expected?

Typically, no one type of data set will give a complete picture of the professional learning needs of staff or the effectiveness of professional learning implementation. For example, stakeholder perception data might show a belief that a school is high performing, but student performance data might show a different result. This is why multiple types and sources of data need to be examined and discussed among stakeholders when making a proactive professional learning plan. Finally, being transparent and sharing data with staff—whether to justify professional learning decisions or to show the growth and improvement that resulted from their hard work—helps to establish trust, motivate staff, and reinforce continual learning.

See Table 5.1 for examples of qualitative and quantitative data that can be collected in various professions.

Table 5.1. Data Examples

Professional field	Quantitative data examples	Qualitative data examples
Teaching	Standardized test scores, attendance records, graduation rates	Parent surveys with open-ended questions that ask for written responses, student interviews, samples of student work
Nursing	Average time patients spend in recovery; number of patient falls, infections, or injuries; number of hours spent with each patient	Patient surveys about quality of care, performance evaluations
Law	Statistics about case outcomes (wins and losses), number of times lawyer contacted client, number of ethical complaints	Client satisfaction surveys, peer reviews about quality of work produced, comments in ethical complaint
Real Estate	Time taken to respond to phone calls, time listings spend on the market, total number of homes sold, number of hours worked (full time or part time)	Surveys from past clients about their home buying/selling experience, recommendations on social media

Chapter Six

Proactive Professional Learning Trait #3

Job-Embedded

"That's when I first learned that it wasn't enough to just do your job, you had to have an interest in it, even a passion for it."—Charles Bukowski, *Factotum*

"An authentic test not only reveals student achievement to the examiner, but also reveals to the test-taker the actual challenges and standards of the field"— Grant Wiggins

One of the main principles of adult learning (see Chapter 2) is that adults are more motivated to learn when the learning is relevant to their daily lives and clearly connected to their future goals and ambitions. Professional learning will be most relevant to professionals when it is integrated into their day-to-day practice. The third essential trait of proactive professional learning is that it is job-embedded, meaning that it is applied on the job to address authentic, work-related problems, as opposed to taking place in a classroom or environment that is removed from the professional context.

Job-embedded professional learning is different from on-the-job training (OJT), although it can certainly include OJT. OJT training is achieved when employees engage in hands-on learning of professional skills on-site, as opposed to classroom learning. Research shows that trainees who receive structured OJT demonstrated increased motivation and better performance than trainees who only received classroom training. Structured OJT has a positive effect on achieving organizational objectives and financial outcomes.

However, not all learning needs to take place on the job for it to become job-embedded; there is a wide range of high-quality learning experiences (such as conferences, webinars, and self-directed action research) that are not OJT because they are disconnected from the workplace, but the learning can become job-embedded with the right planning and supports.

For professional learning to be job-embedded, time must be built into the workday for professionals to learn and apply research-based or industry-accepted practices in authentic contexts, to collaborate with colleagues and engage in reflective dialogue, and to receive feedback from knowledgeable peers or leaders. Teachers, for example, must be able to observe, practice, and regularly discuss with colleagues research-based instructional practices for facilitating learning in children. The concept of job-embedded professional learning can be easily transferred to other industries; practices that have proven to be effective in a profession and align with industry-driven standards can be applied in context regularly and with support from employers and colleagues in a system that was designed with job-embedded professional learning in mind.

Making professional learning job-embedded requires significant planning since it involves establishing an organizational culture of continual learning. Organizations that establish and maintain a culture of learning encourage a variety of professional learning opportunities and provide operational flexibility to ensure planned time and schedules that accommodate staff in collaborative reflection on their practice.

First, organizations will need to establish core values that promote a collaborative and supportive learning environment. They will need to develop routines and policies that provide professionals with the time and resources (meeting space, technology) for interdepartmental and cross-departmental collaboration and reflection dedicated to problems of practice.

In addition, organizations will need to build leadership capacity so that there are staff members who can serve as professional learning facilitators and models of effective practice. These designated leaders would not only be highly skilled and accomplished in their professional practice, but they would also need to be trained in adult learning principles, strategies for effective group collaboration skills (establishing group roles and norms, interpersonal communication, conflict resolution, active listening), and proper implementation of the professional learning models such as those covered in Chapters 8–13.

In the teaching context, formal teacher leadership positions would be created for master teachers who have demonstrated expertise in effective teaching practices. Teacher leaders would remain in the classroom for part of the school day, but serve in a leadership role for part of the day to help build professional competence among other teachers. This practitioner-leadership model could be applied in all other industries as well. Distinguished professionals could remain in the practitioner roles for a portion of the workday but also have designated work time to serve as professional learning facilitators.

SUPPORTS FOR JOB-EMBEDDED PROFESSIONAL LEARNING

An organization's proactive professional learning plan can help organizational leaders and the practitioner-leaders who will guide job-embedded professional learning to strategize how the various training methods, such as webinars, workshops, and book study groups, could be combined with *supports* that would enable staff to implement new knowledge on the job.

Coaching

Perhaps one of the most important supports for sustained, job-embedded professional learning is an effective coach. The expectation of the coach is to observe and provide timely and specific feedback to the employee or team. Coaching provides differentiated support based on individual needs. Coaches can model the new learning and, when needed, deliver additional training and professional development to the employee or team based on the data obtained from the observations.

The role of the coach is to support employees through reflective dialogue, not to evaluate or manage, so an effective coach must have the ability to develop trusting relationships (Knight, 2009; Toll, 2005).

Professional Learning Communities

An essential point about expecting organizational change from professional learning is that the focus cannot be solely on the individual; there must be systemic support for the individuals who are learning, growing, and working within the system. In the education world, a professional learning community (PLC) has been a means for addressing the systemic supports needed to foster individual and collective growth because it is "an ongoing process in which educators work collaboratively in recurring cycles of collective inquiry and action research to achieve better results for the students they serve" (DuFour, DuFour, Eaker, & Many, 2006, p. 11).

Although they originated in schools, PLCs that are focused on common goals of personal and organizational improvement can be incorporated in any industry.

In addition to having common goals for professional improvement, PLCs are based on shared accountability. All members are accountable to one another in the sense that they are committed to accomplishing team goals, and they are all accountable to the end users of their services (students, patients, customers, clients). A PLC that is serving its purpose will have the following qualities:

- There are clearly defined goals for improvement that align with organizational goals.
- There are protocols and processes for collaboration and interaction.
- Discussions are focused on data and evidence of effectiveness of practices.

Through PLC, colleagues can regularly and purposefully investigate problems of practice, share data-informed strategies and solutions, and support one another in developing their expertise. Coaching and PLCs as supports for professional learning will be further discussed in Chapter 7.

Chapter Seven

Proactive Professional Learning Trait #4

Continual

"In short, you can't let the deadline define the mission. The mission has to define the duration."—Richard Holbrooke

"We must use time wisely and forever realize that the time is always ripe to do right."—Nelson Mandela

Industries are constantly changing, and practices learned just a few years ago may no longer be relevant today. When continual, lifelong learning is not a priority, professional practice can become stagnant and outdated. But beyond inevitable changes in the professional landscape, we know definitively that people learn differently from one another. The amount of time it takes a person to learn something well enough to perform it in practice will vary by the individual due to a number of reasons: prior knowledge and experience, interest and motivation to learn, and biological factors.

While research on professional learning cannot give an exact number of hours that professionals must spend learning a new skill, one thing is clear: short-term, time-inflexible learning experiences cannot be expected to produce lasting results. Research indicates that professional learning that results in improvements in teachers' instructional practice, which in turn produce improvements in student learning outcomes, is intensive and *ongoing*, or *continual*.

In studies that have shown demonstrated improvement on student success from teacher professional development, the workshops or seminars that the teachers attended were either intensive and long term (four weeks), or they were supported with regular, ongoing follow-up activities afterward (Yoon, Duncan, Lee, Scarloss, & Shapley, 2007). Yet, when a need for important skills arises in the workforce, organizations still provide sporadic and disconnected trainings to staff, such as webinars, conferences, and short workshops, which are by themselves insufficient for improving professional practice. Even if the training is high quality, demonstrates evidence-based practices, and is targeted toward an organizational goal, it is unlikely to be effective if the participants are unable to properly implement the practices on their own after the training.

A proactive professional learning plan will account for time, resources, and supports for continual and individualized learning so that staff can transfer their new knowledge to new contexts while receiving ongoing feedback from knowledgeable colleagues. Reflecting on feedback and adjusting practice accordingly are what will lead to long-term application of knowledge in practice.

SUPPORTS FOR CONTINUAL PROFESSIONAL LEARNING

The same supports described in Chapter 6 to make professional learning job-embedded are also supports for making professional learning continual: coaching and professional learning communities (PLCs).

Ongoing, individualized support from coaches—experts in the field who are already implementing the skills in the professional setting—is essential for increasing the likelihood that staff will be able to properly implement high-quality, evidence-based practices learned in professional learning activities. Creating a professional learning opportunity that includes theory, demonstration, practice, and coaching will increase the duration of time needed for successful implementation.

According to one study of teacher professional development, approximately 95% of teachers who participated in staff development implemented the new skills in the classroom when they were provided with modeling and regular coaching, as compared with 10% when effective modeling and coaching were not provided (Joyce & Showers, 2002; Knight, 2009). To maintain efficacy in staff development, coaches must also engage in continual learning in professional expertise and effective coaching practices.

PLCs as supports for professional learning have a "pervasive and ongoing impact on the structure and culture of the school" or organization (DuFour et al., 2006, p. 10), and participants are committed to continual learning and improvement. A benefit of regular participation in PLCs is exposure to multiple perspectives and sources of feedback. When professionals take time to meet, review data, engage in problem-solving, and reflect on what works and does not work for them, they can evolve together in a culture of lifelong learning. Refer back to Chapter 6 for more information about PLCs.

Not to be confused with a PLC are *communities of practice*, also called *communities of practitioners* (CoPs). A CoP is similar to a PLC in that a group of people get together to continually learn. The big difference between these two learning communities is the PLC tends to focus on the employees or people within the organization as a necessary part of conducting business, but a CoP can include any voluntary stakeholder with an interest in the learning or the topic of focus.

For example, if a school has a CoP on improving literacy, members of the CoP could include people within the organization, like teachers, principals, and staff, but it could also include external stakeholders, like students, parents, college professors, or anyone else interested in the topic or with expertise in the topic. The roles of attendees can also change regularly within a CoP, with some wanting to be more involved at certain times and not involved much at other times (e.g., not attending a meeting but asking to get the notes via email).

Whether the supports are coaching, PLCs, or CoPs, these types of post-training supports can assist in extending the duration of the professional learning, aligning individual needs and goals with organizational goals, and continuing to build staff efficacy. Organizational leaders should assume responsibility for establishing a culture that supports continual application of and reflection on knowledge gained from professional learning activities; core values should reinforce continual learning, and structured time should be built into the workday for collaboration.

On the other hand, when a culture of lifelong learning is established, the responsibility of improving practice can fall more on the individual. When employees believe in the need for continual improvement and are intrinsically motivated to grow as professionals because they see the importance of their work to others, they will find ways to do so on their own and share their knowledge with others. The employees themselves can be initiators and leaders of professional learning and supports.

Chapter Eight

Conferences and Workshops as Professional Learning

"A diversity of thought, perspective and culture is important in any field. . . . Surround yourself with people who support you."—Sarah Friar

"Interacting with others keeps me motivated, clarifies information and extends understanding."—Douglas Fisher

Some of the most energizing moments of a career come from hearing an expert or experts share insights about our profession and remind us why our work is important. These energizing moments spark new and rich conversations with the diverse individuals who have dedicated themselves to a chosen field and open us to new thoughts and perspectives.

CONFERENCES

The potential for networking, exploring the latest products from vendors, and bringing fresh ideas and inspiration back to a place of employment are among the many reasons why attending conferences is a desirable option for professional learning. A conference is a scheduled event, usually a full day or multiple days, with an agenda that includes keynote speakers and multiple breakout sessions in the form of presentations, workshops, or seminars.

One downside of sending staff members to conferences is the cost. For example, if a conference registration fee is $750 per person, and the company is sending four people, that registration cost is $3,000. Additional travel costs can range from approximately $100 to $7,000 depending on whether the conference is local or whether the participating staff members need airfare, ground transportation, overnight accommodations, and meals. Having the four people in this scenario attend a conference to participate in a handful of 60- or 90-minute sessions could cost the organization up to approximately $10,000. Some leaders might find it more feasible and cost-effective to have local presenters or trainers come to provide targeted information to all staff on-site rather than expend the resources on a few individuals.

Another issue to confront regarding conferences is that learning activities at conference sessions are short in duration (often under two hours), the quality may be inconsistent (there might not be active participation), and employers do not have any control over the content covered, so making the learning targeted, data-driven, job-embedded, and continual will require additional work from participants afterward. The motivation from the conference speakers will not likely be sustained after the source of the motivation (the conference) disappears.

By itself, conference attendance is not effective in making long-term change. Planning between leadership and the attending staff members should occur prior to the conference to solidify expectations. The staff members who attend the conference can be asked to further investigate relevant practices that align with the organization's goals to see how they can be embedded in the unique setting of the organization, implement those practices on the job, and facilitate a professional learning activity for other staff members. The process could look like this:

1. Staff members who want to attend a conference provide justification and data linking the topics covered at the conference to organizational needs and goals.
2. Staff members and leadership review the conference agenda together and identify sessions that align with organizational goals. The attending staff members commit to collecting information about and implementing a new practice that is targeted to an organizational improvement goal. Before signing off on the expenses for the conference, leadership might consider whether what the staff will learn is sufficiently aligned with the organizational goals and whether the organization can realistically support application of the new initiatives discussed.
3. Staff members work with leadership to identify ways to build capacity within their organization using the knowledge they bring with them from the conference. They might lead an action research team, facilitate a workshop, or allow others to conduct observations of them implementing the new practices.
4. Staff members and leadership identify supports that will be needed to implement the learning activities identified in number 2. They might need work time to conduct further research, meeting space to deliver instruction, and training on facilitation and coaching skills.

Gathering as much information about the conference up front will prevent wasted resources from sending staff to learn about practices that the organization is not prepared to implement. Other information to gather includes the following:

- *Location*: Is the conference in state, out of state, or even out of country? If it is out of the state, will the content still apply to your agency's certifications, state laws, practices, or working guidelines?
- *Time*: What is the date of the event, and when does the event start and end each day? Do the times and dates interfere with other job responsibilities or prior commitments?
- *Cost*: What is the all-inclusive cost of this event (travel, food, registration, materials, lodging, time away from work, and energy to get all resources together)? Is the total cost justifiable, or is there a more cost-effective way for staff to learn about the topics?
- *Topic tracks*: Are the sessions organized into "tracks" or specific categories? Are the tracks aligned to the professional learning needs of your staff and organization?
- *Outcome*: How will attending this event ensure improved system growth and employee practices, and how will the learning align to organizational outcomes?
- *Speakers*: Who are the specific speakers for each session, and does their expertise make the learning opportunity valuable?
- *Networking*: Will attendees have the ability to brainstorm and mingle with others in your industry?

Using this proactive approach, organizations can maximize the investment in professional learning activities while allowing staff members to take on leadership roles among peers. In addition, more ambitious professionals will be inspired to present at conferences, building their professional reputation while representing the organization.

WORKSHOPS

Workshops are structured meetings led by a facilitator that can include guided learning, group discussion and problem-solving, hands-on activities, and formative feedback. They can occur on-site or off-site and be led by external consultants or staff members who have demonstrated expertise in the targeted skills and knowledge. Workshops vary in duration from a day to several weeks. Benefits of workshops include the ability to target learning content to the specific needs of the participants, time for collaboration with colleagues around problems of practice, and the opportunity to practice skills and receive feedback from a knowledgeable trainer.

Historically, workshops have been used as one-shot events, sometimes called "drive-by" or "pray and spray" professional learning. Unless the workshop is intensive and sustained over a considerable period of time (several days or weeks), studies show it will be less effective or ineffective in leading to improvement. Studies of teacher professional learning indicate that more than 14 contact hours are needed to show a significant positive effect on student learning (Yoon et al., 2007). Single-day workshops are common, but, like conference sessions, they will need to be followed with long-term, job-embedded supports for the learning to be properly implemented on the job.

HOW CAN CONFERENCES AND WORKSHOPS BE TARGETED, DATA-DRIVEN, JOB-EMBEDDED, AND CONTINUAL?

Targeted: Conferences can be targeted if prior to receiving approval to attend at the expense of the organization, participants and leadership review breakout session summaries and choose sessions that address a problem or practices that align with organizational goals. The same applies for workshops that are not developed by members of the organization to address specific organizational needs. Investment in a workshop should be based on how well the workshop aligns with organizational priorities, as evidenced by the published description, learning objectives, and syllabus or outline if available.

Data-driven: Conference and workshop attendance can be data-driven if prior to receiving approval to attend at the expense of the organization, participants are able to use data to demonstrate how the learning can benefit the organization. As part of the professional learning plan, staff should be asked to justify how attending a conference or workshop will help to fulfill organizational needs as evidenced by the data. One support that leadership must consider in a professional learning plan is that staff might need some assistance from leadership in obtaining the necessary data. Leadership should make appropriate data accessible to staff members seeking professional learning opportunities, or use the data to justify requiring staff participation.

Job-embedded: The materials or information from most conferences and workshops, such as handouts or booklets, might be beneficial during the event, but without some sort of additional connection to the work setting and job duties, that handout or booklet can easily collect dust on a shelf. As part of the professional learning plan, participants should be asked to explain how they can help to transfer their learning to the job setting and share it with others.

This might be difficult to do based on workshop descriptions and session summaries alone, and the plans can adjust as needed, as long as participants are aware of expectations to implement the learning in professional practice after the event. Even if the topic of a conference is something that can benefit the employee in the workplace, sometimes the specifics of how to embed the skills to the individual's unique setting won't be clear. Supports—such as additional learning activities, coaching, and professional learning communities (PLCs)—need to be provided within the professional learning plan.

Continual: Conferences and workshops have a short-term time frame, usually one to three days in length, although some intensive workshops can run for weeks. Alone, conferences and short workshops do not meet the criteria of being continual. Any motivation attendees gain from conference attendance can quickly wane if there is no reinforcement planned post-conference or workshop. If the topic is important enough for implementation on the job, additional learning activities and supports (coaching, PLCs) should be accounted for in a professional learning plan so that learning is ongoing.

Chapter Nine

Observation as Professional Learning

"You cannot hope to sweep someone else away by the force of your writing until it has been done to you."—Stephen King

"It's all about paying attention. Attention is vitality. It connects you with others. It makes you eager. Stay eager."—Susan Sontag

From the moment of birth, human beings learn by observation. The learning theories discussed in Chapter 2 show how we never stop learning from watching others, and we learn from other people's responses to our actions, which can ultimately either reinforce or modify our behaviors. The people within an organization are a rich resource that can be tapped for building the knowledge of others through observation practices. Observation is an opportunity for colleagues to collaborate and help one another grow as professionals in a comfortable, non-threatening arrangement.

For the purposes of this chapter, there are two methods for using structured observation as professional learning. One method is *learning-by-observing*, in which the observer is the learner—a professional who has an identified professional learning need. The observer is paired with another professional who has demonstrated expertise in the targeted area to observe best practices performed on the job. The other method is *peer observation*, a reciprocal process in which participants are peers who take turns observing each other to help the other improve practice. In peer observation, the observer observes a peer performing an on-the job task and provides targeted feedback, so the peer being observed is the learner.

MAKING THE RIGHT PARTNERSHIPS

An essential part of effective structured observation as professional learning is that the participants are well matched. Leadership can assist in matching participants by having staff members fill out a self-assessment survey that will help to identify professional strengths and learning needs. In addition, other sources of data should be considered, such as past performance evaluations and end-user data (e.g., student achievement data).

Based on this data, participants should be matched whenever possible according to their unique strengths and weaknesses so that they can assist each other in achieving their individual learning goals. In the learning-by-observing method, the participant who needs to strengthen targeted areas for growth can be matched with an expert practitioner who excels in those particular areas.

In reciprocal peer observation, participants should be logically matched to maximize the potential for constructive feedback that leads to lasting change in professional practices. If two co-workers are allowed to choose each other as partners because they like each other, but they are both novices in the same important professional skills, then the peer observation process is not likely to lead to significant improvement because the partners are not equipped to provide useful feedback in those particular areas.

STAGES OF STRUCTURED OBSERVATION

Unlike observations from a manager for performance reviews or consideration for a promotion, observations for professional learning are not evaluative or judgmental in nature. They are based on trust and mutual respect between two professionals sharing practices and engaging in reflection for self-improvement. Learning-by-observing and peer observation have similar structures and protocols for observation, but the roles of the participants are reversed.

Observation as professional learning is most effective when it is structured and well planned. The participants should receive instruction about their role in observation, observation etiquette, and the steps of the peer observation cycle (outlined below) that they are committing to perform. The process can break down if participants believe they are conducting an evaluative observation and provide judgmental feedback, or if participants perform only some but not all necessary steps. There are five stages of observation: pre-observation, observation, post-observation, reflection, and implementation.

1. Pre-observation

In the *pre-observation* stage, the participants meet to establish rapport, discuss the focus of the observations, and set boundaries, such as the amount of time the observer will stay. In the learning-by-observing method, the observer will determine the focus of the observation because it is the observer who is seeking to improve professionally.

In the peer observation method, the person being observed will determine the observation focus because he or she is seeking feedback on performance in specific areas. In both cases, the participants defining the focus of the observation should be basing decisions on learning goals (personal and organizational) and data, such as performance evaluations and end-user data (e.g., student achievement data, client satisfaction data, etc.). See Chapter 5 for more information about using data to determine learning goals.

Engaging in thorough self-evaluation prior to the pre-observation meeting is an important responsibility for participants so they are well prepared to establish a clear focus for observation. What exactly is the point of the observation? What targeted knowledge and skills will be the emphasis of the

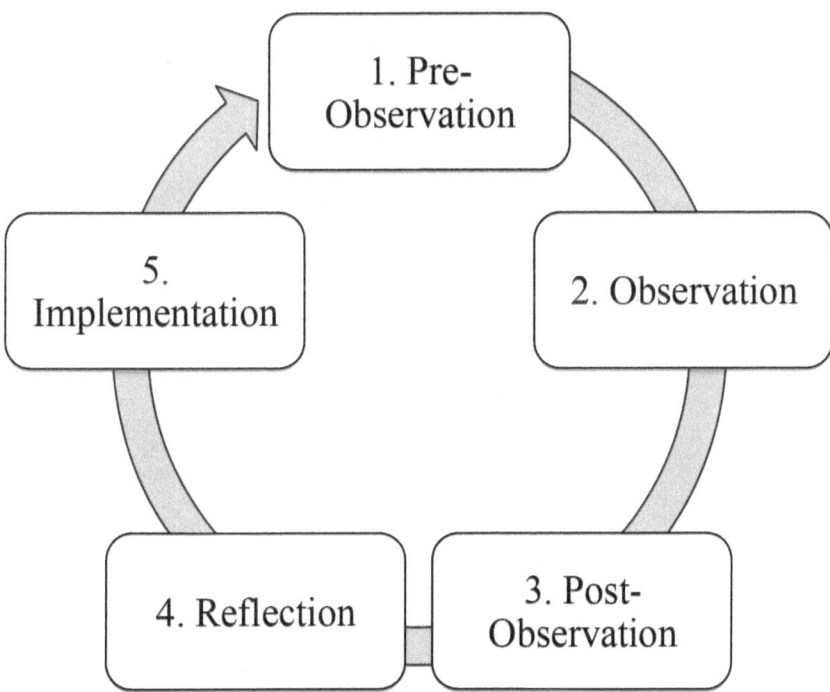

Figure 9.1. Observation Stages

observation? How should the observer enter the workspace to minimize disruption? As with any professional learning activity, the more focused and targeted, the better the chance of positive results.

A checklist or feedback form can be created using notes from the pre-observation conversation. Tools such as checklists and forms will be important in keeping the observer focused on the targeted skills and practices and will ensure that evidence is collected to support feedback. See Table 9.1 for examples of observation tools.

2. Observation

The second stage is when the actual *observation* occurs. The observer should follow the agreed-upon observation etiquette and protocols, such as when, where, and how to enter the workspace. Based on the criteria agreed upon during the pre-observation, the observer takes detailed notes using a tool (as described in the pre-observation stage) that keeps the feedback or questions focused on the targeted area or areas. If the observer is there to give feedback, it will be important for the observer to collect evidence to support feedback. The observer should collect evidence of practices that are going well to reinforce them as well as practices that could be improved. If the observer is there to watch and learn from an expert, then the observer should take detailed notes about what they observed and have questions ready to ask at the post-observation meeting.

Typically, the observation should be kept confidential, and thoughts about a colleague's performance should be shared only with the colleague during the post-observation conference unless involvement of leadership was mutually agreed upon to assist the participants in their learning.

Table 9.1. Examples of observation forms

Sample from a learning-by-observing form:

Targeted skill	Evidence of this skill during observation (What specific actions demonstrated this skill?)	Questions about what I observed	Plan for implementation (How can I apply what I observed in my own practice?)

Sample from a peer-observation feedback form:

Targeted skill	Evidence of implementation (What was done well? How do you know?)	Suggestions for improvement using evidence (I noticed that . . . One thing you could try is . . .)

3. Post-observation

After an observation is complete, participants meet in a *post-observation* conference. Prior to the conference, the observers review their notes and prepare questions and comments. This stage will be different between the learning-by-observing method and the peer observation method because the purpose for the comments and questions will be different.

Peer Observation Follow-Up

In a peer observation cycle, the observer reviews observation notes, prepares positive and constructive feedback—meaning that feedback addresses areas of strength and areas for improvement in a positive way—supports the feedback with evidence, and prepares any questions for the observed party. An example of positive feedback from a teaching observation is, "The way you asked students thought-provoking questions to get their attention before reading the story was effective because the students seemed interested to read." An example of constructive feedback is, "I noticed that a couple of students get fidgety and distracted during the lesson. One suggestion I have is to put students in groups for a hands-on activity to keep everyone engaged."

The peer observer can also come to the conference prepared to ask open-ended questions that allow the observed peer to reflect on decisions made during the observation. For example, the observer watches the peer have a phone conference with an angry client and makes notes about the tone the peer used with the client on the call. A yes/no question could be, "Was your intention to get nasty with the client?" This type of yes/no question carries judgment, which is one way to make the peer defensive and cut off any trust. Another example could be, "What was your point in being curt with the client at the end of the call?" Although this is an open-ended question, it still comes across as judgmental. A better open-ended question would be, "I noticed your voice change toward the end of the call. How do you think the client perceived your tone?" This is an inquisitive question that minimizes judgment. Based on the peer's answer, the observer can then offer suggestions that are more targeted to the observation goals.

Learning-by-Observing Follow-Up

In the learning-by-observing method, the observer is there to learn from an accomplished professional (who may or may not be a peer) and not give feedback, so providing feedback and asking questions that have a developmental or evaluative intent would be inappropriate. In this case, the observer will review observation notes to ask open-ended questions that will serve to clarify the learner's misconceptions or provide additional information needed to implement new knowledge and practices on the job. For example, if the observer, a newly licensed accountant, is watching an experienced accountant work with a client, the question could be, "I noticed you advised the client to create a new limited liability company (LLC) instead of inheriting an existing one. What was it specifically about the client's circumstances that made you feel that was the best approach?"

The time frame for the post-observation conference to occur should not exceed a week, as the experience and memories from the observation need to remain fresh and as clear as possible to both the observer and observed partner. If the post-observation conference occurs more than a week after the observation, recollections of the event can become vague.

At the end of the post-observation conference, participants can plan for next steps. When it is time for the learner to implement new practices, will the partner be there to observe and provide feedback about implementation? In the case of peer observation, the answer is most likely yes, and the implementation observation should be planned and scheduled. In learning-by-observing, it may or may not be the observed experienced practitioner who comes to observe and provide feedback about the learner's implementation of new knowledge and skills; in this case, the observer might be a coach or leader instead.

4. Reflection

After the post-observation conference comes the *reflection* stage. During reflection, both the observer and the observed partner separately reflect on the experience and the process. What was learned from the experience? What parts were rewarding and what parts could have been better?

The observed partner in peer observation can reflect on how the positive feedback will reinforce current practices and how the constructive feedback can be used to revise practices. The observer can reflect on the quality of the feedback and evidence he or she provided to the learner and what changes might be made in future observations. The observer can also reflect on successful practices observed that he or she might adopt to use in his or her own practice.

In learning-by-observing, the observed practitioner can reflect on how well he or she was able to answer the observer's questions to facilitate learning. The observer can reflect on new ideas and practices that were discovered during the observation, how the learning can be implemented on the job, what additional learning or supports are needed to continue to improve, and what might be done differently next time (e.g., quality of notes taken or questions asked).

5. Implementation

Both types of observation cycles end with an *implementation* stage. The learner in either observation method will use input from observation notes, the post-observation conversation, and personal reflection to implement new strategies and practices that resulted from the observation experience. Implementation of new knowledge and skills occurs on the job in the authentic professional context.

It should be expected that the learner may not be immediately proficient in implementation of new knowledge and skills. It might take several performances with constructive feedback to get comfortable using new practices. This is why someone knowledgeable should conduct an implementation observation—whether it is the partner in peer observation or a coach or practitioner leader for the learning-by-observing method—and provide feedback to help the learner refine skills in practice. In this way, the observation cycle continues until the learner is proficient in targeted skills and practices.

HOW CAN PEER OBSERVATION BE TARGETED, DATA-DRIVEN, JOB-EMBEDDED, AND CONTINUAL?

Targeted: Structured observations are not just aimless visits to a colleague's workspace that result in questions and comments about anything that was observed. During the pre-observation conference, the participants communicate the focus of the observation, which should be a specific target area or areas for improvement for the individual that also align with organizational goals. The participants can create tools to keep the observation focused and targeted, such as checklists or rubrics.

Leaders can assist in making peer observation activities targeted by pairing up observation partners according to areas of need. Leaders who know the individuals and their needs for development can suggest partnerships in which partners can complement each other's strengths and target areas for improvement. For example, if one teacher struggles with classroom management, a principal or department chair will pair that teacher with one who excels at classroom management. But remember that peer observation is supposed to be voluntary and non-threatening, so if for whatever reason some people are not comfortable working together, they should not be forced to.

Data-driven: Observation participants should use data when identifying areas for improvement. For example, a teacher might look at past performance evaluations, student learning data, or classroom behavior trends to determine what areas need attention to better serve the students. Because reflection is a key part of the peer observation process, participants should be collecting data during implementation and reflect on the data to see what is working and what the next steps should be.

Job-embedded: Observation is job-embedded by design because the observation occurs in the work setting. A challenge for job-embedded observation is time. Time needs to be built into the workweek for employees to conduct observations and attend the pre- and post-observation meetings. In addition, employees who participate in observation may need training on the specific structure and protocols of observation and other necessary skills such as collaboration, interpersonal communication, and providing supportive and useful feedback.

Continual: Observation is not intended to be a one time event, although without planning it can easily become one. The cycle (pre-observation, observation, post-observation, reflection, and implementation) should occur over a prolonged period of time and can be repeated when necessary. Just as attending one conference session will most likely not lead to sustained improvement, neither will completing one observation cycle. Repeating observation cycles to gather feedback about implementation of new learning allows for continual improvement.

Chapter Ten

Book Study as Professional Learning

"The more that you read, the more things you will know. The more that you learn, the more places you'll go."—Dr. Seuss, *I Can Read with My Eyes Shut!*

"Literature is the safe and traditional vehicle through which we learn about the world and pass on values from one generation to the next. Books save lives."—Laurie Halse Anderson, *Speak*

Book discussion groups fulfill several needs for those who participate: a need for new information and mental stimulation, a need for community and camaraderie, a need to discuss and reflect on ideas, and the list goes on. When using book study as a form of professional learning, an additional benefit is improved professional practice and outcomes for the end user of professional services.

In book study for professional learning, participants read and discuss a book, journal, or article related to theoretical and practical professional contexts that can increase their understanding of best practices as well as enhance their professional effectiveness. Usually, the entire staff or department reads the same piece of literature so they can have structured, focused conversations to target an organizational learning goal. Book studies can create a collaborative and engaging learning experience for multiple employees that will continue to be referenced long after the book study has concluded.

Book study is more than just assigning all staff to read a book; it requires advanced planning for it to be effective in improving professional practices. This planning includes these steps:

- choosing the right book,
- deciding how often the team will meet to discuss the book,

- determining how much of the book participants will be expected to read for each meeting (reading and discussing in chunks can help ensure everyone is "on the same page"),
- planning logistics of book study conversations and delegating facilitation tasks, and
- planning for how and when participant reflections and on-the-job implementation of book information will be documented.

CHOOSING THE RIGHT BOOK

Picking the right book for a book study is an important first step because choosing the wrong book can be alienating or boring to staff or counterproductive to what the organization is trying to achieve. Even if the book has multiple five-star ratings on book review sites, it is still a good idea to preview the book to make sure it is a good choice for the staff and the intended purpose of the book study. While someone in leadership will end up selecting the book to ensure that it aligns with organizational learning goals, inviting staff suggestions for consideration or narrowing down options to a few choices and allowing staff to vote on the winner can increase staff buy-in and engagement in the process.

One way to identify a potential book is to look at professional organization websites to find book recommendations. Many professional organizations will have a "Resources" or a "Publications" section on their website that could contain potential book study materials. For example, in the educational field, groups like the Council for Exceptional Children will recommend to their members books that are focused on different areas of special education. Another idea is to browse the texts being used in college or university classes pertaining to the area of focus. Simply asking others in the field if they have read any recent literature that focuses on the desired topic can also lead to some fitting choices.

ASSIGNING THE READING: DECIDING HOW MUCH AND HOW OFTEN

The length of the selected book and the difficulty of the reading are important considerations in planning for book study. Depending on how much time is being set aside for the book study, if a long book is selected, maybe only important portions of the book can be read and analyzed within the time frame provided. For example, if the book study is to take place over three months with the team meeting once a month for two hours a meeting, a realistic assessment will have to be made about how much content can be read and discussed in detail within those time constraints.

Although it may be difficult to avoid having team members who do not read the book or who skim through the reading at the last minute, the book study discussions are reliant on team member participation and commitment. When members do not have time to read and reflect on the reading, the discussion can become derailed when participants answer discussion questions with information that is irrelevant to the book. Not only is this frustrating to the team leader and the members who did read the book, but it also wastes meeting time.

Chunking the reading appropriately and assigning digestible portions for busy professionals over manageable time intervals so that they can actually think deeply about and not just gloss over important information will make the book study discussion more meaningful and productive. Reading assignment decisions should be informed by the varying ability levels of participants, the goals and outcomes of the book study, the type of book assigned (e.g., a peer-edited research journal compared to a personal memoir), and the depth of the questions the team will be using to analyze the text.

Once a realistic reading schedule is determined, leadership can assist by reminding team members what they are supposed to read and by when. For example, if 30 pages of reading is expected within a month, the leaders can send out a friendly email or direct message to team members 15 days into the month reminding them that in two weeks the team will be meeting to discuss the reading. The same reminder can be sent out a few days prior to the meeting. These small check-ins will help team members make the reading a priority and fit it into their other personal and professional responsibilities.

FACILITATING THE DISCUSSION

Before teams can meet to discuss the reading, logistics need to be taken care of. Leadership will want to ensure that meeting space is adequate for the discussion. If the entire organization is meeting face-to-face, smaller groups will need to be established with participants assigned, and there need to be multiple rooms available. Seating arrangements should be conducive to group conversation; participants should be able to comfortably see and hear one another and have a desk or tabletop accessible so they can underline the book and take notes on a pad of paper or a laptop.

If the book study takes place online, leadership might still need to create separate discussion "spaces," such as different conference calls or web links, if the number of total participants is too high for a structured discussion in which everyone can participate. The online facilitators of book study discussions will also have to ensure other members have the time to read the comments of others and respond accordingly. A major planning consideration is that all team members who lack technical skills in online meetings are given training ahead of time so that they are comfortable with the online environment and understand the discussion protocol and expectations.

The questions the team discusses should be written and approved prior to the meeting because they need to be explicitly and purposefully tied to the professional learning goal the book study is intended to address. In some cases, the leader or facilitator will create the questions, but in other situations, the team members might collectively design the questions to discuss, or trade off the responsibility after each meeting. Whoever develops the discussion questions should have carefully read the reading and should have substantial knowledge of the goals for professional and organizational improvement that the reading supports. The questions are the core of the discussion, so if the questions are weak, a weak discussion can be expected to follow.

Closed-ended questions, which can be answered with a simple yes or no answer, should be avoided since they do not allow for in-depth discussion. If a closed-ended question is used, make sure to probe with the follow-up question, "Why?" The questions should be thought-provoking and promote critical thinking. They should challenge participants to clarify what they have learned in their own unique way and justify their points of view.

Although the book study might begin with factual questions (who, what, where, or when), the quality of the discussion will come from questions that analyze the book's content. These questions can help participants categorize the new information with information they already know or use, discuss how the new information can have an impact on their work and the organization, hypothesize about how the information could change their work or how the organization functions, and brainstorm about what additional information is still needed to apply what was covered in the reading in daily practice. Questions can be handed out when the reading is assigned so participants can read the text with an understanding of what will be discussed when the book study team meets.

Last, the facilitator will need to ensure all in the book study have had multiple opportunities to participate in the discussion. Prompts like, "For the next question, let's begin with someone who hasn't replied yet," or "Stacy, I know this topic is crucial to your work. Any thoughts on what we just read?" can help the facilitator involve everyone in the book study and hold everyone accountable for the learning.

PARTICIPANT REFLECTIONS AND IMPLEMENTATION

Reflection on the reading and discussion should occur shortly after the discussion. Participants can just freely reflect, but guiding questions can help participants to focus their reflection on how the reading and discussions caused them to reevaluate their practices, how the new knowledge connects or conflicts with their prior knowledge, and how the new knowledge and skills can be used in practices to achieve organizational and individual professional learning goals. The reflection can be done as a group and in private journals using "I used to think . . . but now I think . . ." types of prompts.

From the beginning of the book study initiative, it should be clearly communicated that some aspect of the learning is expected to be implemented in practice and that the new knowledge and skills should lead to action. Working with leadership, participants can create an action plan in which they commit to implementing a new practice based on the learning from book discussions and then sharing with the group the outcome of implementation at the next book study or staff meeting.

Combining the action plan with another professional learning model or support, such as peer observation or coaching, reinforces the learning and increases the likelihood that high-quality implementation of new practices will endure over time. The action plans and the outcomes of the action plans should be documented to show a timeline of what the team accomplished as well as evidence that reflection and implementation resulted from book study participation.

HOW CAN BOOK STUDY BE TARGETED, DATA-DRIVEN, JOB-EMBEDDED, AND CONTINUAL?

Targeted: Making a book study targeted to organizational improvement and professional learning goals begins by carefully selecting a book that will inspire and prepare participants to work toward those goals. Some books tackle multiple issues and topics, and in this case the book study planner and facilitator should focus on the chapters or sections that specifically address the targeted learning goals and avoid getting sidetracked by the irrelevant content. The discussion prompts and questions, when carefully crafted, will serve to keep the group's focus on improving professional practice in specific areas tied to organizational improvement.

Data-driven: Book studies should be based around a text that tackles a problem that data has shown to be an issue at the job setting or in the field. For example, if perception data shows that collaborative and supportive relationships are lacking in a work environment, then a book study on building relationships or conflict management would be a data-driven choice. Also, if staff are attempting to implement what they read, then bringing the data from their implementation experience to the book study discussion is using data to refine new skills until they are integrated into regular practice.

Job-embedded: Book studies become job-embedded when they occur during the workday and when participants implement an action plan based on the book study. Action planning can be a collaborative activity, and individuals can seek input from peers in a book study group for transferring learning into practice. Time should also be provided during the workday for participants to share their experiences implementing book study learning and reflect on what can be repeated in the future and what needs to be done differently.

Continual: Book studies can be continual when participants meet in intervals while reading the book (after each chapter or natural stopping point), not just once when the book is completed. Notes or graphic organizers can also be provided, so once the book is finished, the participants will have the key points for future reference. Finally, the action plan for implementation makes the learning continual, especially when it is combined with other models and supports, such as peer observation or coaching. Having knowledgeable colleagues observe implementation and provide feedback encourages long-term positive changes in professional practice.

Chapter Eleven

Action Learning as Professional Learning

> "There is a void in our psyche that can be filled only when we are solving challenges, designing solutions, developing products, opening markets, innovating processes, and creating jobs."—Randy Gage, *Mad Genius: A Manifesto for Entrepreneurs*

> "As you navigate through the rest of your life, be open to collaboration. . . . Find a group of people who challenge and inspire you, spend a lot of time with them, and it will change your life."—Amy Poehler

In the summer of 2018, 12 boys and their soccer coach became trapped in a cave in Thailand and were at risk of drowning if heavy rains caused flooding in the cave. Volunteers of various nationalities and areas of expertise—from divers to paramedics to engineers—joined forces to help find a solution that would result in the best outcome: bringing the group out of the cave alive and well. This is just one example of how urgent problems can be solved when knowledgeable individuals work together to achieve a goal.

Action learning is a professional learning process in which a small group of professionals work on a problem or need that affects the entire organization, act to address the problem or need, and reflect on their learning both collectively and individually. Action learning, therefore, not only provides professional growth for participants, it also actively addresses an issue for organizational improvement that improves outcomes for the end users who rely on the organization's services. Organizations develop leaders through action learning because participants can lead colleagues in questioning their own assumptions about their profession and applying the strategies developed in the action learning process to effect system-wide change.

While investigating a problem can be performed by an individual alone, the action learning process is fundamentally collaborative. Multiple perspectives are needed to get at the heart of what the problem truly is, how it affects the organization as well as the individuals, and what potential, perhaps unexpected, and innovative solutions can benefit the organization and all stakeholders, rather than solutions that reflect the needs and biases of one individual.

THE ROLE OF INQUIRY IN ACTION LEARNING

For the team to arrive at innovative and creative solutions to organizational problems, participants must be open-minded. They should not begin the action learning process with preconceived notions of what is causing the problem or how the problem can most effectively be solved. Openness to substantial change and collaborative inquiry are necessary qualities of action learning teams.

Inquiry is an ongoing process of asking questions to find answers to a problem. During action learning team meetings, the team will begin to ask questions such as these:

- What has been done in the past, and how do current practices contribute to the state of the organization?
- Who is affected by the problem and how?
- What are the root causes of the problem?
- How can we improve individually and systematically to solve the problem?
- What have we overlooked, and how can we do things better?
- What data support the decisions we have made?

The group's dialogue around the questions that participants ask generates potential solutions to be tested. Between team meetings, team members should be putting ideas into practice, recording results, and collecting data that might help to answer questions or raise more questions. As questions and insights about the problem and the solution arise, it is important for the team to document their journey, both for their personal gain and also to explain to decision-makers how they got to their conclusions and solutions. Realistically, there will be "bumps in the road" that will provide excellent opportunities for the action learning team to revisit and refine their thinking.

THE ROLE OF REFLECTION IN ACTION LEARNING

The *learning* aspect of action learning relies on the team's ability to reflect on their action learning journey, both as a team and as individual team members. Team members are expected to journal on their progress to reflect on what has been accomplished, what questions the team still has, and what new learning has occurred at the individual, team, and organizational level.

At the individual level, reflection should focus on individual skills. For example, participants can identify personal areas of growth or strength that were developed while working through the action learning process, such as collaboration skills, leadership skills, or professional content knowledge. Within the reflection, the participant can brainstorm next steps for applying and reinforcing their learning in professional practice, and even building capacity among their colleagues in those areas.

At the team level, the reflective learning should focus on the team dynamic. How is the team doing as a whole, and what has been learned through the process that can be applied to future team endeavors? What systems were put in place to make this team function that should be repeated in future meetings and that can assist when future teams are formed?

At the organizational level, the reflective learning should focus on building capacity among staff to create a culture of continual learning and improvement. For this to happen, how will the results of the action learning be shared with others, and if effective, how can the results of the action learning shape the policies and procedures of the organization?

It is recommended that one team member should serve as a coach to assist the action learning team in processing their thinking and making sure that team members are continually learning from their experience (Marquardt, 2002). The coach monitors the group conversation to identify learning moments, record lessons learned to be applied in future discussions, prompt members to reflect, and ensure that learning gets shared system wide.

HOW CAN ACTION LEARNING BE TARGETED, DATA-DRIVEN, JOB-EMBEDDED, AND CONTINUAL?

Targeted: The action learning team should come up with a problem worth solving at an individual, team, and organizational level, which creates three areas of targeted focus. If the problem is not targeted enough, the team will realize the ambiguousness of their goals and issues as they begin going through the action learning process.

Data-driven: Just like any other professional learning goal, the focus of an action learning team should be based on multiple sources of data showing that the problem being investigated is a priority for the organization and has a significant impact on the end user. Data is needed to justify why this issue deserves to be the focus of the action learning team. Because reflection is a key part of action learning, the individuals and team members are continually collecting data to determine whether new practices are effective and what the next steps should be.

Job-embedded: Action learning is job-embedded by design. Because the problem is one that affects the organization, it should naturally be embedded within the work of those tackling the issue. Time must be built into the workday for team members to meet, research, collect data, and reflect. Between meetings, team members will be testing new practices on the job and collecting evidence of effectiveness, which will require participation from co-workers.

Continual: The process of action learning is continual because a significant problem will take a significant amount of time to comprehensively address. The cycle of action learning is ongoing as the team meets to explore and design strategies and solutions, applies the strategies on the job and evaluates results, and then meets again to reflect and ask more questions. Proposed strategies will be tested and evaluated, and then the group will reflect and adapt as needed. The adaptations will then need to be applied and evaluated in a continual cycle. In addition, there will always be new problems to solve once a past problem is successfully addressed.

Chapter Twelve

Individually Guided Learning as Professional Learning

"Individual commitment to a group effort—that is what makes a team work, a company work, a society work, a civilization work."—Vince Lombardi

"If you don't know, the thing to do is not to get scared, but to learn."—Ayn Rand

Although the importance of collaborative learning is stressed in the professional learning literature, some people prefer to learn alone, and they achieve more when they are free to determine their own learning path. Most likely, there will be staff members who already have demonstrated expertise in professional practices that are the focus of system- or department-wide professional learning activities, and these individuals need an alternative option to be challenged and to grow professionally. *Individually guided learning,* a model in which learners determine their own professional learning goals and select the models and activities to help them meet their goals, is ideal for independent and self-directed learners.

Individually guided learning is not a good fit for all staff members. Although it is desirable due to its flexibility, it is only likely to be successful when the participant has proven dependability, has demonstrated commitment to learning and self-improvement, and possesses strong independent research and planning skills. A major drawback of this model is the lack of collaboration, and, therefore, the lack of multiple perspectives that cause people to challenge their own thinking. The motivation learners get from social support systems for accomplishing goals is also lacking, so the individuals who choose this route for professional learning tend to be self-motivated.

The role of leadership in individually guided learning is to monitor the progress of participants in completing these essential steps:

- Selecting challenging goals that address an individual learning need and align with organizational improvement goals
- Creating a plan of action to achieve the learning goals
- Documenting the completion of all learning activities committed to in the plan of action
- Completing assessments to demonstrate learning, often in the form of a portfolio or video recording
- Reflecting on the experience and sharing learning for the greater good of the team and the organization

Unless participants are required to share their knowledge, others in the organization will not benefit from individually guided learning. Organizations that want to maximize the investment in professional learning might have stipulations that participants using work time and resources to pursue individually guided professional learning are required to share their knowledge and facilitate others' learning.

This model provides motivating opportunities because professionals who drive their own research can use it to create products of their learning that can not only build capacity within the organization but reach beyond the organization to a wider professional audience, such as presentation proposals for national conferences and papers to submit for publication. Getting published in peer-reviewed journals is one avenue for contributing to the professional conversation and having a greater impact on others' learning.

If peer-reviewed journals are too intimidating, many industries have professional organizations that publish blogs from guest or freelance writers that are shared widely on social media. An Internet search can produce leads for getting published on less formal professional platforms. A well-researched topic that has relevance to a professional audience could potentially get published and shared, promoting the reputations of both the author and the organization.

HOW CAN INDIVIDUALLY GUIDED STUDY BE TARGETED, DATA-DRIVEN, JOB-EMBEDDED, AND CONTINUAL?

Targeted: Although the individual learner determines the learning goals and delivery models, the learning should support organizational as well as personal learning goals. A coach, mentor, or leader can assist the individual in ensuring the problem is targeted enough to have clear goals and success criteria.

Data-driven: Learning goals and topics of study should be determined using multiple sources of data. Because periodically documenting and sharing their professional learning journey with someone is a best practice for individually guided learning, participants will collect data about the process.

Job-embedded: While in the process of the self-directed learning journey, participants should be testing out practices on the job and reflecting on their effectiveness. The research performed as a learning activity should inform professional practice, and experiences implementing the learning should be documented as part of the learning plan and assessments. Combining individually guided learning with other models (such as observation) or supports (like coaching) provides the participants with opportunities for feedback on their application of learning on the job.

Continual: Individually guided study is continual if the learning goals and activities are challenging and take time to research, practice, and reflect on. The products created as a result of the learning can contribute to others' professional growth within and outside of the organization if participants are ambitious enough to submit them for publication or for presentations.

Chapter Thirteen

Mentoring as Professional Learning

"Everybody's gotta learn, nobody's born knowin'."—Harper Lee, *To Kill a Mockingbird*

"I've been around a long time, so I guess I've touched a lot of people's lives—hopefully for the better."—Ace Frehley

The word *mentor* can mean different things to different people. To some, a mentor is just a knowledgeable person who is available when questions arise. To others, a mentor is a role model. For professional learning, formal mentoring is a program that supports a partnership between an experienced, accomplished professional, *the mentor*, and a novice or someone less experienced in the profession, *the mentee*. This partnership focuses on on-the-job development of the mentee's professional competence. A mentorship is a non-evaluative relationship that is built on trust, collegiality, and confidentiality.

A majority of Fortune 500 companies have some type of mentoring program in place because of the demonstrated benefits to employees and the organization. Both mentors and mentees derive significant benefits from a mentorship. The benefits for the mentee are more apparent because the mentoring model was created to improve outcomes for novice employees. Those outcomes should include increased competence in job performance, increased confidence in professional skills and judgment due to having a support system, easier acclimation to a new work culture, and emotional support when facing challenges. However, mentoring is a professional learning experience for the mentor as well. Benefits for the mentor include these:

- *Growing as an expert*: Yes, mentors are already considered masters of their craft, but even masters can continually improve, and guiding others in professional practices causes mentors to reflect on and refine their own.
- *Becoming better communicators and collaborators*: In a well-established mentorship program, mentors go through training on effective communication skills to establish a supportive, non-evaluative relationship with the mentee. The mentor must also communicate with administrators and supervisors but for the purposes of being able to develop the mentee in a way that supports a shared organizational vision and goals while still maintaining the confidentiality of the mentorship.
- *Changing the lives of others*: Not only does being a great mentor possibly change the course of a mentee's career because he or she was not left isolated in a new environment to learn by trial and error, but the end users of the mentee's practices also benefit from the mentor's involvement. If the end users are students, this means that the mentor makes a difference in the students' learning because their teacher had a mentor to guide teaching practices. If the end users are patients, the mentor can significantly influence their health by mentoring his or her nurse or other healthcare professional.

Developing more competent and confident employees, whether veterans or newbies, is a worthwhile investment for employers, which is why mentoring is a popular professional learning model in schools and the business world.

One important consideration for mentoring is that while every novice can benefit from having a great mentor, not every experienced and accomplished professional should be a mentor. Expertise in the field is only one qualifier for being a mentor. Passion for the profession and for sharing knowledge with others are equally important traits. So are openness to receiving training and learning new skills, willingness to collaborate, and patience and flexibility with adult learners. Mentors should receive intensive training on critical mentoring skills such as forming appropriate and productive relationships; providing useful, non-judgmental feedback; and maintaining confidentiality, just to list a few.

Although mentoring programs will vary from organization to organization, there are five basic steps that are common in the mentoring model.

Step 1: Establishing a Relationship

The first few meetings between a mentor and a mentee are so important because the success of the whole process will be dependent on establishing mutual trust and respect. The responsibility for leading the initial conversations really falls on the mentor because the mentor will have received training on process and protocols while the mentee might not have received much information about what to expect.

The first meeting should be focused on getting to know each other. The mentor and mentee can discuss professional goals and aspirations as well as hobbies outside of work. The mentor will want to emphasize that conversations are confidential and that the mentee is not being evaluated by the mentor.

Step 2: Negotiating Expectations of Each Other

Once rapport has been established between the mentor and mentee, expectations need to be communicated. The roles of the mentor and mentee will most likely be outlined in documentation from the place of employment, so there will be some consistency about what mentorship is and is not. The established protocols should be discussed so that everyone is in agreement about what each party is and is not responsible for. Beyond the basic boundaries provided by the organization, there will be flexibility about how mentoring will occur. Both parties should agree on when, how often, how long, and where the two will meet. Will it be once a week for one hour in the mentor's office? Or every other week for two hours in the company cafeteria? What happens if someone needs to reschedule? How should that be communicated?

Step 3: Targeting Needs

Beyond the practical elements of the mentorship, expectations that are specific to the mentee's development, such as areas of focus for improvement, need to be identified, and the mentor and mentee should work together on creating a plan to target those specific areas. Important tools for identifying the mentee's learning needs will be self-evaluation surveys (strengths and weaknesses are self-identified), reflection logs, and other documentation that the mentee collects as evidence that the mentor can review to provide guidance. Another useful source of information will be evaluation observations from a leader or manager, if the mentee has had one yet.

Step 4: Career Development

A mentor's job is ultimately to help the mentee develop and refine professional strategies until they have successful results. To accomplish this objective, a mentor can ask the mentee guiding questions and discuss strategies; however, the mentor should also be willing to go beyond talk and actually model strategies that have worked for him or her in similar situations.

Giving the mentee timely and constructive feedback is important, especially when the mentee has questions about whether he or she performed a task correctly or responded appropriately to an unexpected situation. Both parties will need to be adaptable during this process. In real life, new variables get introduced on the job that can change an employee's job responsibilities and, therefore, their areas of need for development. The mentor should also be ready to be available to the mentee during unscheduled time, since unforeseen difficulties may arise, and the mentee may need urgent input from a mentor.

Step 5: Sustaining the Relationship

When does the official mentoring relationship end, and what is the role of the mentor and mentee after the fact? In many cases, a mentorship officially lasts around six months to a year, and then formal structure ends but the relationship continues naturally in a "you know how to find me if you need me" or "my door is always open" situation. There are other scenarios that provide a more gradual release after the official mentoring requirements end, which can include less frequent meetings and/or changing the communication preference.

For example, in the second year of the mentorship, instead of meeting face-to-face each month, participants email each other and meet face-to-face on an as-needed basis. It all depends on the chemistry between the individuals and their comfort level with each other. Some mentor-mentee relationships last a lifetime!

HOW CAN MENTORING BE TARGETED, DATA-DRIVEN, JOB-EMBEDDED, AND CONTINUAL?

Targeted: Mentors work with mentees on specific areas of improvement, and they communicate with leadership to understand how areas of focus are aligned with the organization's vision and improvement goals. Mentees must grow not only as professionals but also as members of the system in which they work, so the job of the mentor is to guide the mentee in successfully refining skills not only for the mentee's benefit but also for the benefit of the organization and the end users.

Data-driven: Data (from self-assessments or observations, e.g.) are used to identify areas of focus for the mentee's development. Mentors and mentees review data together to examine practices and determine what is and is not working. Strategies that mentors provide to mentees to improve practice should also be evidence-based practice for the profession.

Job-embedded: Mentoring, when implemented correctly, is naturally job-embedded because the mentor and mentee are focused on refining the mentee's knowledge and skills as they are applied on the job. They will review together the mentee's documentation and reflection on work experiences when developing strategies for improvement.

Continual: Mentoring relationships are intended to provide ongoing support for new or struggling staff members, often lasting for months or years. In mentor training, commitment to keeping regular meetings and check-ins should be stressed to maintain a consistent and continual mentorship. The mentor should be proactive in keeping open lines of communication rather than waiting for the mentee to ask for help.

Chapter Fourteen

The Proactive Professional Learning Plan

Putting All the Parts Together

"Every system is perfectly designed to get the results it gets."—Paul Batalden

"Remember, if you fail to prepare you are preparing to fail."—Reverend H. K. Williams, *The Biblical World* (1919)

PUTTING THE PLAN TOGETHER

Sifting through all of the literature about adult learning theories and professional learning models and practices can be overwhelming. Organizational leaders might know the necessity of having coherence between the staff development that an organization invests its resources in and the organization's areas of needed growth, but they may struggle to put all the pieces together to achieve that coherence.

The proactive professional learning plan (PPLP) is a system that synthesizes what research has shown to be most effective in teacher professional learning and implementation science that can be applied in any field. The PPLP consists of five interconnected parts (see Figure 14.1) that can occur linearly within the cycle but can also move back and forth fluidly as needed when parts need to be revisited, since things often will not go according to plan and adjustments will be needed.

Chapter 14

THE PROFESSIONAL LEARNING PLANNING TEAM

The professional learning planning cycle for an organization can begin with bringing together a team of stakeholders representing various levels within the organization who have outcome data: leadership, employees, coaches, and any other practitioners who should be involved in improvement efforts. Team protocols should make it clear to all members that the purpose of the team is to use their input to focus on collective learning, growing, and problem-solving.

THE DATA

If the cycle starts with the team, then the next step is when the team looks at data to identify areas of need or growth. See Chapter 5 for explanations of the different types of data that can be used to track success and improvement outcomes. When using data to drive professional learning, it is important to refer to multiple sources of data to ensure there is enough evidence to support the investment.

When selecting data sets to use to identify areas of professional learning, relatively consistent sets across all industries include performance or outcome data, perception data, and process data. These data can include surveys

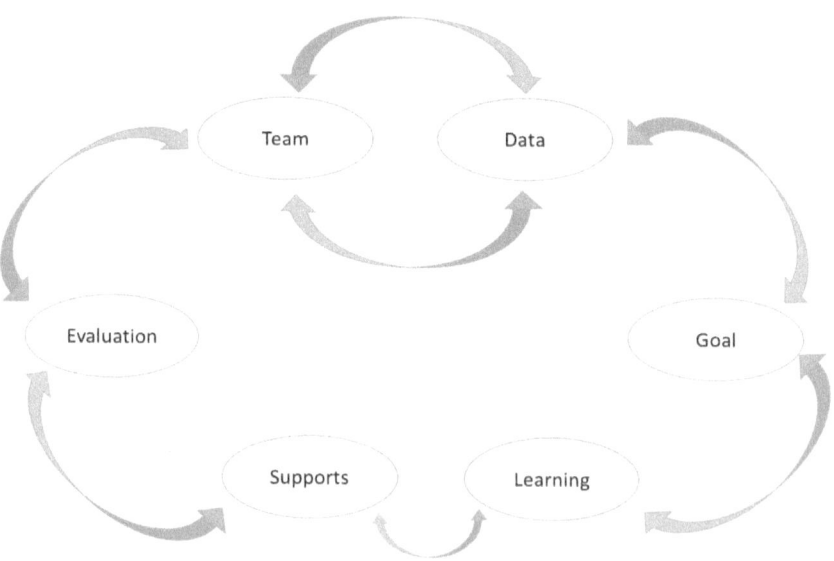

Figure 14.1. The PPLP

from previous professional development opportunities, perception data on how employees feel prepared to do their job, satisfaction data from clients, or achievement data.

Based on the analysis of the data, the team can identify meaningful and important areas to align professional learning opportunities. At this point, the team decides what other stakeholders, if any, need to be brought in to either explain the data, identify additional data that needs to be collected, or decide on courses of action based on the data.

This data also will serve the purpose of creating a baseline or a starting point to note the state of the organization or group within the organization prior to new professional learning being implemented. The baseline data is a crucial part of professional learning evaluation. It will be needed to determine whether professional learning efforts were effective. Ideally, once professional learning has taken place and the new knowledge and skills have been implemented within the organization, the data will show a positive change between the current state of the organization and the baseline data due to a more knowledgeable and competent workforce.

THE PROFESSIONAL LEARNING GOALS

After the team uses data to identify areas of growth, the next step is to create professional learning goals. The professional learning goals will articulate the priorities for measurable behaviors the organization wants to cultivate among staff to provide improved, higher-quality services for the end user.

Following the SMART format will ensure that the professional learning goals are as follows:

- Specific—The goals indicate the specific behaviors that will result from the learning and the individuals who will be affected.
- Measurable—There must be a way to evaluate the effectiveness of the learning in producing the desired results. Progress toward the goal will need to be measured.
- Attainable—It is a realistic goal that can actually be achieved in a specified time frame.
- Relevant—The goal ties back to the organization's needs and priorities.
- Time-Bound—There is a set time frame in which the goal will be accomplished.

Once SMART goals are created, the team should break each SMART goal into smaller learning goals, objectives, or competencies. See Chapter 4 for more information about goals, objectives, and competencies. Using the following organizational SMART goal as an example, what will the smaller

Education	By the next semester, all math teachers will implement problem solving frameworks at the depth-of-knowledge (DOK) 3 and 4 levels in all mathematics units of study as measured by monthly classroom observations during the school year. Benchmark assessment data will be compared to show whether student performance is improving in math tasks that require higher-order thinking.
Health Care	In the next fourteen months, the clinic's wellness program will assist in reducing the percent of patients identified as obese from 25% to 13% as evidenced by body mass index (BMI) calculations.
IT/Tech Support	By the end of the fiscal year, the company's online support unit will successfully customer support and satisfaction by 20% as evidenced by a decrease in 1 and 2 ratings on the satisfaction survey when compared to last year's data.

Figure 14.2. Examples of SMART Goals

learning objectives look like? What smaller pieces of knowledge and skills will the employees need to master to accomplish this goal?

> SMART Goal: By the end of the fiscal year, the online support unit will successfully improve customer support and satisfaction by 20% as evidenced by a decrease in 1 and 2 ratings on the satisfaction survey.
> Learning objectives or competencies:
>
> - Use strategies for establishing positive rapport with customers.
> - Practice active listening to determine the source of customers' complaints.
> - Improve knowledge of systems for more successful and efficient troubleshooting.
> - Successfully apply the stages of the troubleshooting process.

Identifying the smaller learning goals that make up an overarching SMART goal will be extremely useful in the next part of the plan: identifying learning models and supports. The appropriateness of each learning model or support will be determined, in part, by the targeted learning objective or competency, since it is unlikely a single learning model will achieve the entire SMART goal.

THE LEARNING MODELS AND SUPPORTS

Once the team has established professional learning objectives or competencies that make up an organizational SMART goal, the next task is to explore options for learning models that best support development of the identified learning objectives or competencies and best fit the unique needs of the organization and the individuals within it. Chapters 8 through 13 cover multiple professional learning models for the team to explore, and a combination of learning models may be needed to accomplish the professional learning goals and sustained change.

Not every learning model will be practical for every organization, nor will they all be applicable or appropriate for every learning goal. Variables such as fit, cost, time, qualifications, values, and readiness of learners can influence whether a program or practice is a good solution for targeting a professional learning goal. The exploration of these variables allows the team to discuss the capacity of the organization to provide professional learning opportunities and supports, the unique characteristics of the learners involved, the culture of the organization, and the specific nature of the professional learning goal.

Sequencing of Professional Learning Models

The learning models selected in the plan should be targeted toward the smaller learning objectives or competencies that will fit together to encompass the entire professional learning SMART goal. Rather than having sporadic, disconnected activities that are typical of ineffective professional learning practices, the plan should include a coherent sequencing of learning models that builds a bridge to the professional learning SMART goal. Here are some questions to ask at this stage: For each learning model used, what is the goal or targeted learning and how will it connect to the ultimate professional learning goal? In what order will skills be developed and objectives or competencies met? Is there a natural progression of how the development of skills should unfold to ensure the SMART goals will be met? How will learning activities build up so the participants achieve all learning objectives?

The following is an example of the professional learning planning process to this point:

At an elementary school, each grade level meets at the end of a school year to review student learning data for incoming students for the next school year. The sixth-grade team notices that many of their incoming students fell far below grade level proficiencies in the area of writing. This is concerning as their incoming students in past cohorts did not show such a gap between writing achievement and grade-level expectations. Deeper investigation of assessment results shows that the area where the students struggled the most was in providing clear reasons and relevant evidence to support ideas, concepts, or argumentative claims in writing. The sixth-grade team decides that this is an area to focus on across all content areas for the upcoming school year.

The team creates the following SMART professional learning goal: Throughout the new school year, all sixth-grade teachers will implement proven writing strategies into lesson plans as evidenced by a minimum of one writing product per week per classroom.

The sixth-grade team leader recalls getting an email for an upcoming workshop titled Struggling Readers and Writers. The training's description explains that a former three-time Teacher of the Year Award recipient will be walking teachers through proven writing interventions that teachers can use before, during, and after writing instruction. The two-day workshop is in a town a few hundred miles away. The team decides to put in a PD request to their principal to allow two teachers to attend the out-of-town training. The two teachers will then return and spend the next three grade-level professional learning community (PLC) meetings teaching their colleagues the strategies that were learned in the workshop.

After the team members have all been taught the strategies during the PLC meetings, the team will agree on three strategies to use in all the classrooms. The teachers will conduct peer observation cycles as they get through the initial implementation stage of using the selected strategies in their teaching practice. Finally, the teachers agree to bring student writing samples to each grade-level PLC meeting and use the writing samples to evaluate where the writing strategies are making a difference and also to get suggestions from one another when students are not showing the desired growth.

In this scenario, the sequence begins with selected team members attending a workshop and then returning to train their colleagues with the support of PLC time being available. The next step in this sequence is the teachers observing one another in using the new strategies and collecting data to be used as a form of evaluation.

Here is another scenario that demonstrates piecing together different learning models to achieve a professional learning goal:

An organization's improvement team looks at their data and realizes that current marketing strategies are not getting the expected regional exposure. The national marketing campaign does not seem to be garnering interest in smaller, local markets due to low sales in specific communities. The team decides to look into more authentic ways of marketing the product to these communities, and the idea of using micro-influencers as a marketing tool is explored. The team creates the following SMART professional learning goal: By the next quarter, all marketing staff will implement best practices in micro-influence marketing as evidenced by a minimum of five marketing contracts with local community influencers and an increase in local market activity by 10% by the end of the fiscal year.

Some team members are familiar with the concept of micro-influencers, but for others it is a completely new concept. For the team to go into this learning experience with the same prior knowledge, the team leader identifies a journal article on the topic. The learning sequence begins with the team reading the article as a mini-book study and then coming back together in a week to discuss the concept in more detail. When the team returns, they believe that the micro-influencer approach seems like a good idea for the local markets, but their problem is how to identify people who locally use the product and how to partner with these people once they are identified.

The team decides this would make for a great action learning plan; however, since only a few team members will participate on an action learning team, and the process might not yield rewards for some time, all marketing staff will attend a targeted series of webinars about micro-influencer marketing, and they will participate in peer observation cycles. The webinars will focus on the smaller learning objectives of identifying and approaching potential micro-influencers, establishing a formal business relationship, and supporting micro-influencers as they get started marketing a product. These learning objectives will be the focus of peer observations.

In this second scenario, the sequence begins with a mini-book study that leads into an action learning plan. The next step in this sequence is to build in the support systems to keep the learning moving forward. Remember from Chapter 7 that learning requires repeated exposure to new content or skills and feedback from colleagues about the success of implementation. If learners only get exposure to a new skill once, the learners will probably not remember it and most likely will never use it. The right supports will help make the learning ongoing and provide opportunities for feedback and dialogue about what is working in implementing the new learning.

Supports

Once the learning models have been selected, the planning team needs to identify support systems to put in place (if they are not already in place) to support learning and implementation of the learning into daily practice. Supports are the processes that improve staff members' competence to achieve the learning goals or that make the environment more hospitable for the learning to take place and be reinforced. As seen in Figure 14.1, the arrow between the learning and the supports is much smaller than the arrows between the other parts of the PPLP because the learning and the learning supports closely rely on each other.

When determining supports that will be needed to implement professional learning models, two points must first be considered:

1. *Background knowledge of staff*: What will the participants have to know prior to the learning event in order to understand the new information? Is there specific terminology all participants will need to know to understand the learning? How will we find out whether staff have the necessary background knowledge? The background knowl-

edge and current skill level of staff need to be considered when planning for professional learning because a lack of prior knowledge can cause frustration and disrupt the learners' ability to learn a new skill if some scaffolding or supports are not provided. For example, if moderate capability using a specific computer program will be necessary for successful participation in the learning event, then staff who need it should receive some training on the program prior to the event.

2. *Difficulty and complexity of new learning*: The difficulty and complexity of the new learning will affect the amount of effort and time each staff member will need to exert to master and implement the new skills. Supports such as coaching, retraining, or additional time may be needed for some staff members to successfully reach learning goals.

   Supports can also come in the form of modified learning plans. Staff members who are advanced and accomplished in an area and are forced to take the same introductory workshops as the rest of the department even though the learning is well beneath their skill level can become frustrated or disengaged. They will not be given the opportunity to build upon their current knowledge and skills and will therefore not benefit from professional learning time as much as their colleagues. Individualized paths in professional learning should be considered whenever possible to avoid wasting time and opportunity to improve.

The next step is determining the supports that will be needed to make professional learning activities job-embedded and continual. One area to examine is the organization's policies. Do policies need to be created or adjusted to support a culture of continual learning? Are there policies that might create barriers to collaboration and continual learning? Are there existing avenues for collecting data on the effectiveness of professional learning implementation? Are there open lines of communication to support staff through the change process? Does scheduling need to be reorganized to accommodate PLCs? For coaching to be effective, do new positions and titles need to be created, or will there be other incentives for employees to take on leadership positions in support of professional learning? What training do the coaches need to help them be successful in supporting colleagues? Review Chapters 6 and 7 for more information about coaching and PLCs.

These supports are needed to help meet individual needs of participants as they progress through the new learning, and they are needed to optimize the quality and coherence of professional learning activities. In some cases, assistance may no longer be needed, and the supports can be reduced, but they are never removed. If all supports are removed, the chance of the new learning or skills sustaining over time diminishes.

RESOURCES

If growth and improvement are important to an organization, then resources such as money, employee time, building space, and technology will need to be allocated to professional learning efforts. Time during professional learning will take the human effort away from other projects, but should be worth it if the professional learning is increasing the knowledge of the labor force, therefore maximizing the use of capital and increasing opportunities for innovation.

The next step is to identify resources available to devote to professional learning. If resources do not exist to launch the professional learning plan as created, then adjustments will need to be made. Where is the location for the professional learning? Is travel required? What materials need to be purchased? Has time been set aside for collaboration? Are the key people involved given time and space to be involved? Considering the organization's resources often occurs continually throughout the planning process, even before learning goals and models are identified, so that the plan is organized around goals and learning activities that are realistic to achieve.

Finally, when planning for learning models and supports, questions about staffing will need to be addressed. As discussed in Chapter 1, high-performing organizations have specific roles for leading professional learning. They also acknowledge those who are accomplished in collaborative professional learning as leaders of learning among their peers. Are new positions or responsibilities needed to plan, design, and implement professional learning activities or to mentor or coach colleagues?

EVALUATION

Last, a plan for evaluating the success of the professional learning once it is implemented should be in place. Evaluation of professional learning implementation will require collecting data before, during, and after implementation, so it will need to be decided ahead of time what data will be needed, how they will be collected, and who is responsible for collecting and analyzing the data.

A PPLP is an evolving process and ongoing cycle that follows the plan-do-study-act (PDSA) continuous improvement cycle. The PDSA cycle is used as a tool in many different industries for improving quality (see Figure 14.3).

Plan: The professional learning team meets to review data, determine professional learning goals, and select learning models and supports.

Do: Staff engage in the professional learning activities and implement their learning on the job with supports. Data are collected throughout the

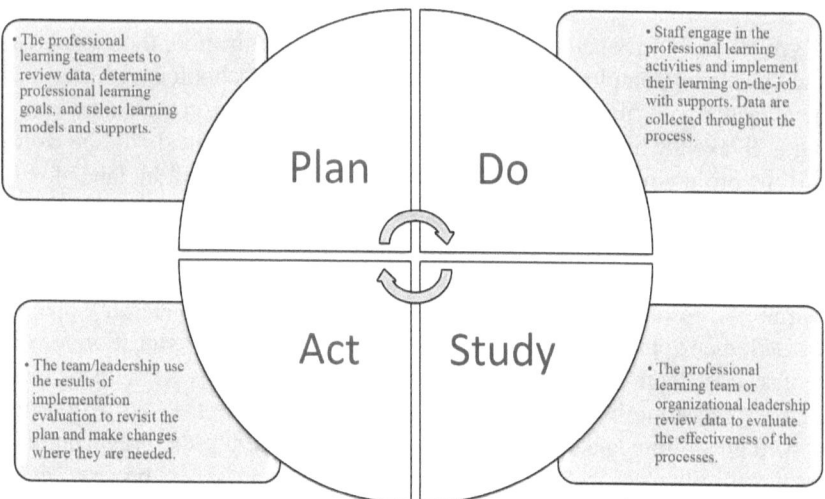

Figure 14.3. Plan-Do-Study-Act (PDSA)

process to document what was done and afterward to determine whether the end user benefited from an improvement in quality as a result of the professional learning.

Study: The professional learning team or organizational leadership review data to evaluate the effectiveness of the processes, identify best practices that should be replicated, and take note of errors to avoid in the future.

Act: The team/leadership use the results of implementation evaluation to revisit the plan and make changes where they are needed.

When planning for evaluation, the improvement planning team should ask, How will we know if they learned it and are implementing it? What tools will we use to determine that they know it and to what degree? The evaluation strategies and tools should provide data that will help the team and participants decide whether the learning experiences were successful or whether some adjustment and reteaching are necessary to ensure all participants are learning. If learning isn't occurring, how can it be corrected? Were the right supports in place? A year from now, what would we show as evidence this worked? What is the evidence we need to start collecting now in order to show this?

A key data point to collect for evaluation is self-reporting from staff to obtain feedback about their experiences. Surveys for staff self-reporting might include these questions: What are you committed to doing this week? What will success look like if you did what you are willing to commit to? In what way will the team track what they are doing to reach the goal and track the journey that was taken to achieve that goal? Is what we are learning likely to improve our work outcome?

Methods for collecting data from the end user (the student, patient, customer, or client) will also be part of the evaluation plan, since the whole purpose of the plan is to improve the quality of professional services. Refer to Chapter 5 for more information about data.

At the end of a cycle, there will be things that work and things that do not work. The goal is to evaluate professional learning implementation so that lessons can be learned from successes and failures and improvements can be made for future efforts. Organizations will struggle to improve professional learning without a plan for evaluating effectiveness.

Recall from Chapter 1 that high-performing organizations also have a system of recognition for achievement and accountability for fixing problems that occurred in professional learning initiatives. How will successes be recognized? How will all members of the organization be held accountable for improving the parts of the processes that fell short? For an in-depth examination of professional learning evaluation, Thomas Guskey's book *Does It Make a Difference? Evaluating Professional Development* (2000) is an excellent resource.

Chapter Fifteen

Change and Resistance in Professional Learning

"Change is the end result of all true learning."—Leo Buscaglia, *Love: What Life is All About*, p. 70

"Nothing is so painful to the human mind as a great and sudden change."—Mary Wollstonecraft Shelley, *Frankenstein*

Having expectations for staff to participate in professional learning is in essence asking them to change. To change their conception of their job and assumptions about their job duties. To change the routines to which they have grown accustomed. To change their mindsets and leave them open to new and different ideas. In the quest for continual organizational improvement, organizations are asking staff to acknowledge that they have areas of needed improvement.

When faced with the call to change, some individuals within an organization will energetically embrace the opportunity to increase their skill set and grow as professionals; this group of individuals will be called the *early adopters*. Many individuals will just go with the flow, neither enthusiastically welcoming nor actively fighting against change; this group of individuals will be called the *drifters* because they are content to drift in the direction of the current without putting too much energy into moving with or against it. Inevitably, there will also be a group of people, the *resistors*, who fear change and try with all their might to thwart it. This group will make change leaders and implementers earn every penny of their salaries.

For all three groups, the reactions to change are normal and should be expected. How many people fall into each group is usually influenced by how much is at stake for each individual by making a change and how much of their world will be transformed as a result of the change.

For example, if a change means some jobs will change more than others, so some employees will have to carry a heavier load than others to adjust to the change, it should be expected that the employees most impacted by the change will resist the change more than others. Alternately, if a majority of employees feel the current state of business is not working, then many of them might welcome the opportunity for change and enlist themselves as early adopters.

Implementing a change such as a large-scale professional learning initiative will never be easy, but knowing how to successfully collaborate with each group of individuals in a professional system is critical to successfully leading continual improvement.

EARLY ADOPTERS

This group will immediately see the benefits of the change or the value of the personal growth that the experience offers. They can become frustrated with colleagues who do not yet see the potential that they see. Early adopters can be powerful allies when they are given leadership roles in the change process. Recognizing their participation in working to achieve a vision can further motivate early adopters. Delegating leadership tasks to them further solidifies their commitment to the change process, and it sends a message to drifters and resistors that some of their peers are on board with the change and it is not just a top-down imposition.

DRIFTERS

The drifters are open to professional learning in the sense that they will show up when it is mandatory and they will not disrupt the process, but they might be a little hesitant about implementing the learning and substantially changing their practices. They might seem indifferent and probably will not go out of their way to participate in a learning opportunity that is optional. For this group, understanding the "why" behind the change is important to gaining their buy-in and commitment to trying new practices. Finding different ways to communicate inspiring messages about why the change is important and how it will benefit employees and the end users can help to make the drifters more engaged and committed.

RESISTORS

The majority of this chapter is devoted to the resistors because they resist change for so many reasons, and they can create serious havoc if their concerns are not adequately addressed and their feelings are not acknowledged. Some resistors will simply refuse or neglect to do what is asked of them; others will push back against the changes and even try to sabotage the new efforts. These folks believe the problem is "out there" and does not involve them because they do not understand why the change is being asked of them. *Emotions and the learning process are interconnected.* Current brain research indicates that learners' emotional state affects their ability to learn (Thompson, 2014). The first step in dealing with resistors is to seek to understand the cause of their reaction.

Here are some common reasons people resist change:

- They are comfortable with the way things are and do not believe any changes are needed.
- They are concerned that the change will threaten their job security.
- They believe that the change being implemented is the wrong change.
- They are interpreting the change as an implication that they have done something wrong and their work is inadequate.
- They have witnessed many failed attempts at change before.

Taking the time to effectively communicate with resistors can make an enormous difference. Those who are comfortable have no motivation to change; in fact, they have motivation to maintain the status quo because they feel safe and happy. Maybe they need to see potential for personal growth in order to be motivated to accept the change. Are there ways that conditions will actually get better for them that they just don't see yet?

For those concerned about job loss, has leadership done enough to assuage these fears and highlight new opportunities for professional growth? For those who believe the organization is making a mistake and implementing the wrong change, has enough information been communicated to staff to alleviate misunderstandings? In addition, has leadership solicited input from staff about the change to give them a sense of being included and invested in the future of the organization?

For those who are taking the change personally and assuming it is a reflection on their performance, well, it might be. But has leadership done enough to establish a culture of continual learning in which everyone shares responsibility for improving practices so that no one in particular feels to blame? Finally, why should the resistors trust that this change initiative isn't just another short-lived dud that will cause a lot of noise and headache but in the end won't make a lasting difference? Perhaps they have seen this before.

Has leadership provided evidence to employees that this change is well considered and data-driven?

The Emotional Struggle of the Resistor

Being a resistor doesn't necessarily mean a person is a bad employee; it just means that he or she is having a negative emotional response to the potential for change. In fact, many of those in the resistor group might be among the most dedicated employees, which is why they are having such a strong emotional reaction to a change.

For many, change is similar to grief because letting go of old habits and patterns feels like a loss. People can become attached to their routines, and when they are forced to change, they can experience the same emotional process as a person who is grieving. The Kubler-Ross Change Curve (see Figure 15.1) shows the stages of grief (Kubler-Ross, 1969). The stages do not have to occur linearly, and individuals can move back and forth between stages. Here, the concept of change in the workplace is applied to the stages of grief.

1. *Denial and/or shock*: This is usually the first stage. People cannot accept that the change is occurring and put up a temporary defense mechanism to avoid acknowledging the change. People in this stage will keep doing things the way they always have, but might start to show a loss in productivity in the workplace. Comments like "But this is the way we've always done things" will come up during meetings and conversations.
2. *Anger*: When the reality kicks in that the change is actually occurring, people can begin to get angry and look for a scapegoat to place blame. People will begin showing their frustration and can appear to be short-tempered with co-workers and family. They might even walk out of meetings in which the change is discussed.
3. *Bargaining*: Once the anger starts to fade, people will often try to compromise or bargain over what parts of that change should and shouldn't happen. Comments like "What if we do this instead?" or "I can do that, but only if I also do this" will occur in conversations. Bargaining is not necessarily a bad thing, as it does signal that people are trying to resolve how the new changes will fit within their reality, and it might even create a solution that benefits all. During this stage, some stress might also begin to be relieved if suggestions are taken into consideration. It is important for leadership to be using active listening during these times and show that the input was received and valued, whether or not it was adopted.

4. *Depression*: In this stage, people might be fearful, regretful, sad, or even feel guilty—that maybe they could have prevented this from happening if they had fought harder. At this point, people might start bringing up all the downsides of the change, and conversations might focus on ways it will fail. Statements like "But what if this happens, then this will be a disaster" or "This one client won't have access to it; therefore, it will be a headache for everyone" will begin to occur in meetings or in more informal forms of communication like gossip or emails.
5. *Acceptance*: Acceptance occurs when people stop fighting the change and begin preparing for it. Some might even get excited about the new opportunities the change is bringing once they have had a chance to mentally process the idea. Energy and productivity might remain low, but as they watch how the change continues to progress, people will get back to normal. There will even come a time when the same people begin to think that this is the way it has always been.

Realistically, this is also the stage where some people might quit or resign from the organization. Some will accept that the organization is no longer a good fit for them and that they belong somewhere else. This is as it should be because the purpose of the change is to increase the achievement of the organization, and team members who will never accept the change enough to help implement it will prevent the team from achieving its goals. Their departure can be seen as a win-win for all involved.

EFFECTIVELY FACING RESISTANCE

When people are resistant to the change, leaders of change implementation can avoid taking it personally and help staff through the process when it is understood that they may be experiencing emotions similar to the grief cycle. It is important to avoid getting defensive when facing resistance because defensiveness can disrupt communication in many ways:

- *Criticizing or snubbing*: "No, that's wrong!" "You just don't understand our vision."
- *Outshining*: "You know these changes will take twice the amount of effort from me than from you." "What you're going to be dealing with is nothing compared to what we're dealing with."
- *Evacuating*: "It's not my job to deal with your arguing or to have to convince you." "This conversation is hopeless, and we are done here."
- *Patronizing*: "Yeah, sure, right, uh-huh." "Well, what did you expect was going to happen?"

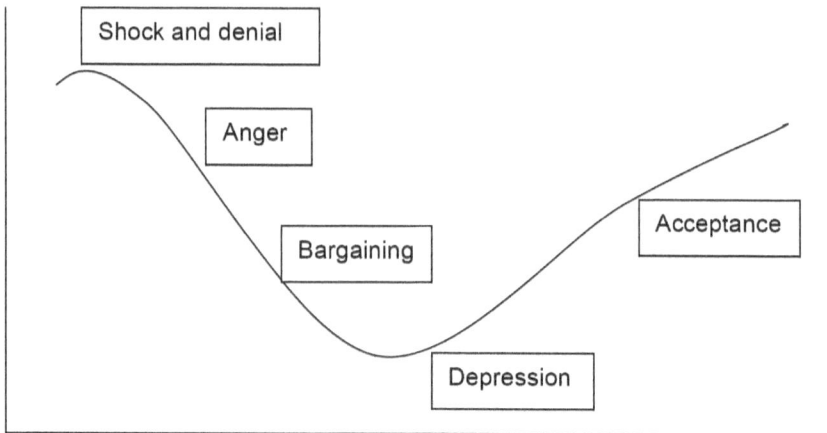

Figure 15.1. Kubler-Ross Change Curve

- *Expounding*: "Check out my résumé. It speaks for itself, so just believe me when I tell you . . ."

Once communication breaks down and rapport is destroyed, then it is nearly impossible to win over resistant staff.

Instead of getting defensive, when dealing with resistors, begin by seeking to understand, then to be understood (Covey, 2004). When seeking to understand where the resistance is coming from, do the following:

- *Clarify*: Ask genuine questions to help understand more fully what is being said.
- *Encourage*: Encourage the speaker by signaling that you are interested and involved.
- *Reflectively Listen*: Paraphrase or summarize what the other person has said.
- *Empathize*: Imagine how the other person must feel.

By proactively preparing to seek to understand, then to be understood, leaders can "reframe resistance to help connect with and persuade the resistors, potentially creating even stronger, more vocal change proponents" (Wright, 2018). If the employee feels that they have been heard and their concerns have been addressed, their energy can begin being used in a productive and positive manner as they move from the resistor group and show as much commitment and enthusiasm as even the early adopters.

USING ADULT LEARNING TO CONSTRUCTIVELY CONFRONT RESISTANCE

Once the implementation of new professional learning has begun, there may be a resurgence in resistance. Adult learners rarely resist learning just for the sake of being difficult. Before taking more managerial steps to combat resistance, such as putting the employees on improvement plans, first look at the implementation of the learning to see if there is a reason for the resistance. When adults resist learning, it is important to reflect on the tenets of adult learning theory (discussed in greater detail in Chapter 2 but summarized here).

- Adults are self-directed learners.
- Adult learners bring rich experiences to the educational setting.
- Adults enter the instructional settings ready to learn.
- Adults are problem-centered in their learning.
- Adults are motivated more by internal factors.

Is the resistance coming from a lack of skill or experience (they don't believe they can do what is being asked)? Is the resistance coming because the individual is not ready to learn new skills and the learner needs some supports? Does the new information go against the experiences the learners are bringing to the learning setting? Is the new learning completely disconnected from authentic problems that the staff is facing, therefore showing little value or purpose in the learning? Any of these factors indicate a learning design problem, in which case it is leadership's responsibility to make sure that adult learning principles are better incorporated into the learning.

SUSTAINING THE CHANGE

Even if the majority of employees in the organization embrace the professional learning opportunity and the changes that will occur, remember that in many cases we are asking people to change behaviors that are difficult to break, and without reinforcement new behaviors can wane. To reinforce the implementation of new learning, keep communication open, track data on the change, and celebrate quick wins. The benefits of the change should be communicated, and the successes should be shared often with all staff so that the new behaviors are reinforced and rewarded.

Celebrating quick wins could be something very simple, like announcing, "I noticed everyone logged into their new accounts this morning," to validate the effort. Quick wins can also have more substance, like "Julie used the new template and mentioned that the workload was less tedious than with the old template. Thanks for sharing, Julie!" Recognizing these quick wins keeps the new knowledge and skills at the forefront of work tasks, and it helps staff to keep a positive attitude about change.

When data become available (e.g., sales data, test scores, or employee satisfaction data) that directly relate to the changes that occurred due to professional learning implementation, share the data and explicitly make the connections between the data results and the changes that have occurred due to the professional learning efforts. For example, if customers or clients write letters of satisfaction to praise services they received after the new learning was implemented, those sentiments—and the credit for producing them—should be shared with all staff.

We all must face change in our professional lives, especially in organizations that are committed to continual improvement, and we will all have emotional reactions to change in various ways. When we are connected to others in a learning community and we are working toward a common goal, we must understand how the change process can affect people differently so that we can work together productively in a strong and collaborative community. The more proactive an organization can be in planning for learning and change, the stronger and more cohesive its learning community will be.

Bibliography

Ahmad, U. (2013). *Impact of training on employee retention.* CASE Business School.
Anis, A. (2011). Employee retention relationship to training and development: A compensation perspective. *African Journal of Business Management,* 5(7).
Archibald, S., Coggshall, J., Croft, A., & Goe, L. (2011). *High-quality professional development for all teachers: Effectively allocating resources.* Washington, DC: National Comprehensive Center for Teacher Quality.
Bandura, A. (1977). *Social learning theory.* Englewood Cliffs, NJ: Prentice Hall.
Blankenship, S., & Ruona, W. (2007). *Professional learning communities and communities of practice: A comparison of models, literature review.* Retrieved from http://eric.ed.gov/PDFS/ED504776.pdf
Blondy, L. (2007). Evaluation and application of andragogical assumptions to the adult online learning environment. *Journal of Interactive Online Learning,* 6(2).
Brinkerhoff, J. (2006). Effects of a long-duration, professional development academy on technology skills, computer self-efficacy, and technology integration beliefs and practices. *Journal of Research on Technology in Education,* 39(1).
Buelow, J. (2014). 3 benefits of making role-play part of training. *Training Magazine.*
Chen, M., (2014). *The effect of training on employee retention.* 2014 International Conference on Global Economy, Commerce and Service Science.
Competency-Based Education Network (C-BEN). (2017). *Quality framework for competency-based education programs.* Retrieved from www.cbenetwork.org.
Covey, S. R. (2004). *The 7 habits of highly effective people: Restoring the character ethic.* New York: Free Press.
Croft, A., Coggshall, J., Dolan, M., & Powers, E. (2010). *Job-embedded professional development: What it is, who is responsible, and how to get it done well.* Washington, DC: National Comprehensive Center for Teacher Quality.
Dalto, J. (2018). *On-the-job training (OJT): An intro.* Retrieved from: https://www.convergencetraining.com/blog/job-training-ojt-intro
Darling-Hammond, L., Hyler, M., & Gardner, M. (2017). *Effective teacher professional development.* Palo Alto, CA: Learning Policy Institute.
DuFour, R. (2004). What is a professional learning community? *Educational Leadership,* 61.
DuFour, R., DuFour, R., Eaker, R., & Many, T. (2006). *Learning by doing: A handbook for professional learning communities at work.* Bloomington, IN: Solution Tree.
Dweck, C. S. (2008). *Mindset: The new psychology of success.* New York, NY: Ballantine Books.
Fullan, M. (2001). *Leading in a culture of change.* San Francisco, CA: Jossey-Bass.
Gallup Institute. (2016). *How millennials want to work and live.*

Gosselin, D. (2017). *Competencies and learning outcomes.* Retrieved from https://serc.carleton.edu/integrate/programs/workforceprep/competencies_and_LO.html

Green, C., & Bavelier, D. (2008). Exercising your brain: A review of human brain plasticity and training-induced learning. *Psychology and Aging, 23.*

Guskey, T. (2000). *Does it make a difference? Evaluating professional development.* Alexandria, VA: ASCD.

Guskey, T., & Yoon, K. (2009). What works in professional development? *Phi Delta Kappan, 90.*

Gutierrez, K. (2017). Mind-blowing statistics that prove the value of employee training and development, *SH!FT.*

Hagel, J., Brown, J., & Samoylova, T. (2013). *Unlocking the passion of the explorer: Report 1 of the 2013 shift index.* Westlake, TX: Deloitte University Press.

Half, R. (2017). *Professional development training: A win for the entire team.* Retrieved from: https://www.roberthalf.com/blog/management-tips/professional-development-training-a-win-for-the-entire-team

Hattie, J. (2009). *Visible learning: A synthesis of over 800 meta-analyses relating to student achievement.* New York: Routledge.

Insured Retirement Institute. (2018). *Boomer expectations for retirement 2018: Eighth annual update on the retirement preparedness of the boomer generation.* Retrieved from https://www.myirionline.org/docs/defaultsource/research/iri_babyboomers_whitepaper_2018_final.pdf

Jagero, N., & Komba, H. (2012). Relationship between on the job training and employee's performance in courier companies in Dar es Salaam, Tanzania. *International Journal of Humanities & Social Science,* Nov.

Jensen, B., Sonnemann, J., Roberts-Hull, K., & Hunter, A. (2016). *Beyond PD: Teacher professional learning in high-performing systems.* Washington, DC: National Center on Education and the Economy.

Joyce, B., & Showers, B. (2002). *Student achievement through staff development* (3rd ed.). Alexandria, VA: ASCD.

Kantar Public and the Learning and Work Institute. (2018). *Decisions of adult learners.* UK Department for Education.

Kilgour, P., Reynaud, D., Northcote, M., & Shields, M. (2015). Role-playing as a tool to facilitate learning, self-reflection and social awareness in teacher education. *International Journal of Innovative Interdisciplinary Research, 2*(4).

Klein-Collins, R. (2012). *Competency-based degree programs in the U.S.: Postsecondary credentials for measurable student learning and performance.* Council for Adult and Experiential Learning (CAEL).

Knight, J. (2009). Coaching: The key to translating research into practice lies in continuous, job-embedded learning with ongoing support. *Journal of Staff Development, 30*(1).

Knowles, M. (1970). *The modern practice of adult education: Andragogy versus pedagogy.* New York: Association Press.

Knowles, M., Swanson, R., & Holton, E. (2005). *The adult learner: The definitive classic in adult education and human resource development* (6th ed.). San Diego, CA: Elsevier.

Kotter, J. (2012). *Leading change.* Boston, MA: Harvard Business Review Press.

Kubler-Ross, E. (1969). *On Death and Dying.* New York: Macmillan.

Learning Forward. (2011). *Standards for professional learning.* Oxford, OH: Author.

Lopes, J. (2017). Self-directed professional development to improve effective science teaching. *Teacher and Teaching Education.*

Marquardt, M. J. (2002). *Building the learning organization: Mastering the 5 elements for corporate learning* (2nd ed.). Palo Alto, CA: Davies-Black Publishing, Inc.

Matthews, P. (2017). How long should a training course be? *Training Journal.*

McGregor, D. (1960). *The human side of enterprise.* New York: McGraw-Hill.

McGregor, D. (1966). *Leadership and motivation: Essays of Douglas McGregor.* Cambridge, MA: The M.I.T. Press.

Mehrdad, A., Salehi, M., & Ali, S. (2009). A study of on the job training effectiveness: Empirical evidence of Iran. *International Journal of Business and Management.*

Miksen, C. (2019). What is the difference between efficiency and effectiveness in business? *Houston Chronicle.*

Mitchell, D. (2012). *Learning through movement and music: Exercise your smarts.* Geomotion Group.

Moss, C., & Brookhart, S. (2012). *Learning targets: Helping students aim for understanding in today's lesson.* Alexandria, VA: ASCD.

National Research Council. (2000). *How people learn: Brain, mind, experience, and school.* Washington, DC: National Academy Press.

The New Teacher Project. (2015). *The mirage: Confronting the hard truth about our quest for teacher development.* Brooklyn, NY: Author.

Pacchiano, D., Klein, R., & Hawley, M. (2016). *Job-embedded professional learning essential to improving teaching and learning in early education.* Ounce of Prevention Fund.

Pew Research Center. (2016). *The state of American jobs: How the shifting economic landscape is reshaping work and society and affecting the way people think about the skills and training they need to get ahead.*

Piercy, G. (2013). Transformative learning theory and spirituality: A whole-person approach. *Journal of Instructional Research, 2.*

Premack, R. (2018). 17 seriously disturbing facts about your job. *Business Insider.*

The Society for Human Resource Management. (2016). *National Study of the Changing Workforce.* Retrieved from https://www.shrm.org/hr-today/trends-and-forecasting/research-and-surveys/Documents/National%20Study%20of%20Employers.pdf

Thompson, R. A. (2014). Stress and child development. *The Future of Children,* 24(1).

Tkatchov, O. (2017). The leaders among us—Mining the leaders in your school. *ASCD Inservice.* Retrieved from: http://inservice.ascd.org/the-leaders-among-us-mining-the-leaders-in-your-school/

Toll, C. A. (2005). *The literacy coaches' survival guide: Essential questions—and answers—for literacy coaches.* Newark, DE: International Reading Association.

Trivette, C., Dunst, C., Hamby, D., & O'Herin, C. (2009). Characteristics and consequences of adult learning methods and strategies, *Research Brief Volume 3, Number 1.* Tots n Tech Research Institute.

Vygotsky, L. S. (1978). *Mind in society: The development of higher psychological processes.* Cambridge, MA: Harvard University Press.

Walsh, B., & Rastegari, I. (2015). *What is knowledge?* Retrieved from www.gse.harvard.edu/news/uk/15/02/what-knowledge

Wen-Rou, H., & Ying-Ju, J. (2016). Comparison of the influences of structured on-the-job training and classroom training approaches on trainees' motivation to learn. *Human Resource Development International, 19*(2).

Wiliam, D. (2016). *Leadership for teacher learning.* West Palm Beach, FL: Learning Sciences International.

Wright, K. (2018). How CEOs Can Win Over The Resistors to Change. *Chief Executive Magazine.*

Yoon, K., Duncan, T., Lee, S., Scarloss, B., & Shapley, K. (2007). Reviewing the evidence on how teacher professional development affects student achievement. *Issues & Answers. REL 2007-No. 033.*

Index

action learning, 15, 53–56
adult learning theory, 8–9, 85

Bandura, Albert, 10; social learning theory, 10
book study, 15, 47–52

coaching, 27, 30
communities of practice (COPs), 31
competency, 18
conferences, 15, 33–35

data: cycle of collection, 21–22; qualitative, 23, 24; quantitative, 22, 24; types, 23

Fullan, Michael, 9

Guskey, Thomas, 22

high-performing school systems, 4

individually guided learning, 15, 57–59
inquiry, 54

job-embedded, 25

Knowles, Malcom, 8; andragogy, 8
Kubler-Ross Change Curve, 82–83

learning forward, 15

learning objectives, 18
learning outcomes. *See* learning objectives
learning targets, 18

mentoring, 16, 61–65

observation: learning by observing, 39; peer observation, 39; professional learning model, 15, 39–46; role in learning, 10
on-the-job training (OJT), 25
organizational goals, 13

PDSA cycle, 75–77
proactive professional learning plan (PPLP), 5, 14, 18, 67
professional learning: benefits of, 2; definition of, xii; essential characteristics of, 14; models of, 15–16, 70–71; proactive, 4. *See also* PDSA cycle
professional learning communities (PLCs), 27, 30
professional learning goals, 17–18

reflection, 55

self-efficacy, 10
SMART goals, 69–70
social cognitive theory. *See* Bandura, Albert, social learning theory

social interaction: role in learning, 9
Society for Human Resource Management (SHRM), 3
supports, 27, 73–74

Theory Y, 13–14, 16

Vygotsky, Lev, 9; sociocultural development, 9

workshops, 15, 35–36

About the Authors

Oran Tkatchov's career has included such roles as a middle school teacher, high school teacher, and charter school director. He has spent the last 15 years directing, presenting, and providing professional development in the areas of special education, leadership, and organizational improvement for various agencies and businesses.

Mary Tkatchov has devoted almost two decades to the education field as a former high school teacher and adult educator. She works in assessment development in higher education. She presents at national conferences and writes articles about education and assessment in higher education.

www.ingramcontent.com/pod-product-compliance
Lightning Source LLC
Chambersburg PA
CBHW030147240426
43672CB00005B/312